THE SPENCER MANSION

South (garden) facade of Gyppeswyk (the Spencer Mansion), 2011: A conservatory once stood at the right-hand corner and a deck ran along the front of the facade, incorporating the porch. The bay window of the drawing room is visible on the right; that of the dining room is on the left. On the second floor are some of the bedrooms, and above them a Palladian window marks the attic level. The original colours were restored in 2004.

PETER REID

THE SPENCER MANSION

A House, a Home, and an Art Gallery

ROBERT RATCLIFFE TAYLOR

Best wishes,
Rob Taylor

TouchWood
Editions

TouchWood Editions
touchwoodeditions.com

LIBRARY AND ARCHIVES CANADA CATALOGUING IN PUBLICATION
Taylor, Robert R., 1939–
The Spencer Mansion : a house, a home, and
an art gallery / Robert Ratcliffe Taylor.

Includes bibliographical references and index.
Issued also in electronic formats.
ISBN 978-1-927129-27-2

1. Spencer Mansion (Victoria, B.C.). 2. Art Gallery of
Greater Victoria. 3. Victoria (B.C.)—Buildings, structures,
etc. I. Title.

FC3846.8.S63T39 2012   971.1'28   C2012-902235-7

Editor: Holland Gidney
Proofreader: Cailey Cavallin
Design: Pete Kohut
Cover images: Spencer family: Image B-02243 courtesy of Royal BC Museum, BC Archives
Art Gallery of Greater Victoria facade: Pete Kohut

We gratefully acknowledge the financial support for our publishing activities from the Government of Canada through the Canada Book Fund, Canada Council for the Arts, and the province of British Columbia through the British Columbia Arts Council and the Book Publishing Tax Credit.

MIX
Paper from
responsible sources
FSC® C016245

The interior pages of this book have been printed on 100% post-consumer recycled paper, processed chlorine free, and printed with vegetable-based inks.

1 2 3 4 5 16 15 14 13 12

PRINTED IN CANADA

To the men and women who created and are
maintaining the Art Gallery of Greater Victoria.

CONTENTS

Detail of an 1889 bird's-eye view of Victoria: At left, on upper Moss Street, the home of Alexander and Theophila Green, Gyppeswyk, is distinguished by its steeple-like belvedere. The Dunsmuirs' Craigdarroch Castle (55) looms above it, while Cary Castle (56) (Government House) lies to the far right. The rural, semi-wooded nature of the area is still evident today.
ELLIS & CO., 1889

THOSE WHO MADE GYPPESWYK THEIR HOME

1889–1899   Alexander and Theophila Green, and their children

1892–1899(?) Frederick and Martha Worlock, and their children

1899–1900   Thomas and Martha McInnes, and their son,
             daughter-in-law, and grandson

1900–1903   Henri-Gustave and Margaretta Joly de Lotbinière

1903–1951   David and Emma Spencer, and their children

1951–1953   Colin and Sylvia Graham, and their son

1953–1977   Several housekeepers and caretakers

THE SPENCER MANSION AS GYPPESWYK?

In 1889, Alexander and Theophila Green named their new home at 17 Moss Street* Gyppeswyk, which is Old English for "Ipswich," after the village in England where they were married and also lived for a while. Later owners David and Emma Spencer renamed it Llan Derwen, which is Welsh for "under the oaks." Today, the house is primarily known as the Spencer Mansion. To honour the Greens, and to avoid confusing readers, however, I refer to the mansion as Gyppeswyk throughout this book. Spellings of this name differ but I've chosen to use the one current at the time of the house's construction, as found in several British sources.

---

* Later renumbered 930 Moss Street. Today, the address is 1040 Moss Street.

Gyppeswyk, *c.* 1890: Earliest known photograph of the mansion, taken in the wintertime, and showing the porte-cochère on the right, the original conservatory stretching from the corner of the east facade toward the main door, the veranda, and the extensive grounds to the south. The different tones on the walls suggest the original colour scheme.

The Spencer Mansion: A House, a Home, and an Art Gallery documents the history of a remarkable Victorian building. For the last sixty years, 1040 Moss Street has been home to the Art Gallery of Greater Victoria. It's an address we are proud of and a place that has been a part of the lives of many generations of Victoria residents.

The history of the Art Gallery of Greater Victoria is tied not only to the building but also to the many volunteers who have ensured its survival and growth as an important visual arts institution befitting the city of Victoria. The most dedicated group of volunteers has been the Gallery Associates, whose actions continue to make an ongoing contribution to the life of the institution.

The efforts of the Women's Committee, which became the Volunteer Committee and later the Gallery Associates, have been fundamental in shaping the gallery. Not only did their foresight create both the Gallery Shop and the art rental program, they also contributed directly to the gallery's permanent collection by either purchasing artworks or donating funds for that purpose. Examples of those works are contained in *Book of Days: Art for Our Time*, which was published in 1998 on the occasion of the forty-fifth anniversary of the Volunteer Committee. It is very clear that these early acquisitions shaped both the collection and the program at the gallery. It is fitting, then, that the Associates mark their sixtieth anniversary with the publication of this book, having operated in the Spencer Mansion for almost as long as the art gallery itself.

The Gallery Associates are very fortunate to have Robert Taylor's involvement and his willingness to take on the task of writing the history of the Spencer Mansion. Robert has a considerable reputation as a historian and an academic, as is evidenced by his research into the social and architectural history of Gyppeswyk.

This publication is the result of the hard work of a number of people. Diane Rickson chaired the Associates' History of the Mansion Committee and worked tirelessly in guiding the publishing process. Diane identified early on the importance of this book to the celebration of the Associates' history and the value of Robert's research. The other members of the committee, Anne Russell, Helen Lantz, Jennie Hurley, and Joan Shimizu, brought their considerable skills and talents to the process. We are all very thankful to Ruth Linka and TouchWood Editions for partnering on this project; they have been most supportive and helpful throughout the process.

On behalf of the art gallery's staff and board of directors, I would like to sincerely thank the author and congratulate the Associates on their sixtieth anniversary.

—Jon Tupper
Director, Art Gallery of Greater Victoria

INTRODUCTION

Gyppeswyk, also known as the Spencer Mansion, is a late-nineteenth-century villa, which now houses part of the Art Gallery of Greater Victoria. It stands on Moss Street at the corner of Wilspencer Place, a block to the south of one of the city's main arteries, Fort Street, and on the border of the Rockland neighbourhood of elegant homes. In 1959, Willard Ireland, then provincial archivist, declared that the house "symbolizes an era, and a very significant era, in the history of Victoria, and, for that matter, of the whole of this province."[1]

At first glance, Ireland's remark may seem puzzling because Gyppeswyk is not the most impressive nor the most well known of Victoria's early mansions. With its soaring towers, Craigdarroch Castle, not far away, is more imposing. In Colwood, Hatley Castle, with its crenellated stone battlements, is larger and has finer gardens. Moreover, because of their British connotations, the neo-Tudor houses of Samuel Maclure and Francis Rattenbury may be more symbolic of Victoria's traditions. In fact, some find the style of Gyppeswyk to be more Yankee than British because of its resemblance to the mansions on Nob Hill in San Francisco.

However, as Ireland implied, Gyppeswyk has a more dramatic history than either Craigdarroch Castle or Hatley Castle, or indeed most of Victoria's heritage mansions, because its residents made important contributions to the commercial, political, humanitarian,

1

and cultural life of the city. The lives of the people who made it their home reflect several aspects of Victoria's history and character. Unlike Gyppeswyk, Craigdarroch Castle was never the home of a married couple with young children. And Hatley Castle (built by James Dunsmuir) was only briefly home to a family. Gyppeswyk, on the other hand, was—for over sixty years—the residence of families: mothers, fathers, children, and, in one case, a grandchild. If its walls could speak, they would disclose hundreds of family secrets, dramas, and comedies. But even though we cannot know all these stories, the house is a vital document of the history of Victoria and, as Ireland suggested, of British Columbia too. As such, it has much to tell us.

In a sense, Gyppeswyk was constructed of gold dust. The house reflects the fact that much of Victoria's early history and architecture grew out of young adventurers' dreams of easy riches. As first constructed in 1889, it owed its existence to the hopes of Alexander Green, a twenty-seven-year-old man hungry for wealth and new horizons. He built it with the proceeds of his fortune-seeking in the gold rushes of Australia and the United States that had lured the ambitious and the brave away from the British Isles in the mid-nineteenth century. Four years after Green's widow vacated the mansion in 1899, it was inhabited by the family of another Briton—David Spencer—who was attracted to Victoria by the Cariboo Gold Rush and who first made his fortune catering to other gold-seeking newcomers and transients. As was the case in many North American cities, Victoria's most impressive mansions were often the result of one man's egotistic need to make a statement about his social status, wealth, and importance. This was probably true of Alexander Green, although possibly less so of David Spencer. At the same time, Gyppeswyk is also a document of the talent, intelligence, and drive of young men who left family and friends in the Old Country to seek their fortune in the New World, in spite of the realization that they would probably never see their hometowns again, and who would make important contributions to their adopted country.

Gyppeswyk reflects Victoria's development and character in other ways too. At the end of the nineteenth century, British Columbia's capital city enjoyed the skills of first-rate architects such as William Ridgway Wilson, who designed Gyppeswyk, and efficient contractors like George Mesher, who actually built it. Moreover, the quality of the detailed woodwork in the mansion's foyer and the ornate plasterwork in its dining room and drawing room suggests that the architect and contractor were able to call upon talented local craftsmen.

Gyppeswyk is also evidence that nineteenth-century Victoria was in no way isolated from at least one dynamic centre of North American life: San Francisco. Not only does the house resemble California mansions, but there are also several personal links to that city: the first owner of the house arrived in Victoria via San Francisco, having first worked and lived there; and several later owners had relatives or business connections there.

Reading about Gyppeswyk's history reminds us that all human beings are supposedly only removed from each other by a maximum of six degrees of separation. Until recently, in Victoria that separation was only one or two degrees. It is just a slight exaggeration to say that in late-nineteenth-century Victoria everybody knew everybody else, at least among the middle and upper classes. For example, the Greens, the builders and first owners of the house, and the Spencers, its later and more famous owners, originally lived across the street from each other in the James Bay area. The sons and daughters of these members of the commercial class went to school together, gave concerts together, and played sports together. Other connections among Gyppeswyk's families are less significant but nevertheless surprising. For example, three of the house's male inhabitants studied and/or practised medicine before entering the different careers for which they became famous. As well, the Greens and the Spencers were typical of local immigrant families in that they helped their relatives get established in the New World, a not uncommon phenomenon in Victoria and elsewhere. Theophila Green invited her sister and brother-in-law, Martha and Frederick Worlock, to come to Victoria, where Frederick joined the firm of Garesche Green & Co. Around 1890, a young woman who may have been one of Alexander Green's relatives served as a temporary governess to the young children living at Gyppeswyk. And David Spencer provided employment for his sister-in-law in his department store.

Evidence of the esteem with which Gyppeswyk was held in official circles in British Columbia was its selection in 1899 as the province's Government House. For four years, it served as the residence of the lieutenant-governor and was thus the site of ceremonial functions, including a gala banquet for visiting royalty in 1901. Gyppeswyk, however, was never a staid, sombre place. During the occupancies of the Greens, the Worlocks, and the Spencers, the mansion reverberated with the noise and bustle of young people, including teenagers. Even during the brief residency of Lieutenant-Governor Thomas Robert McInnes and his wife, Martha, the house was shared with their son and daughter-in-law—and their little boy. As late as 2011, the presence of a clothesline pulley affixed to an oak tree near the northwest corner of the mansion attested that, for more than sixty years, the house was a home to parents and their children—in one case, a grandchild, and briefly in 1953, a newborn baby. Furthermore, as Willard Ireland noted in 1959, "there was always someone living in this home interested in the cultural life of the city."[2] Appropriately, the last function held in Gyppeswyk when it was a private dwelling was Sara Spencer's reception for the Victoria Symphony in 1951. In one way or another, various kinds of music, as well as the visual arts, poetry, and Shakespeare, were cultivated by the Greens, Worlocks, McInneses, Lotbinières, and Spencers—not to overlook the first curator of what is now called the Art Gallery of Greater Victoria, Colin Graham and his wife, Sylvia.

Finally, the fate of Gyppeswyk in the later twentieth century is a reflection of our changing awareness and practice of heritage conservation. Damaged by additions made in the 1950s, the mansion has since been partially and carefully restored to close to its original condition. Today, the house is among only a few examples of late-nineteenth-century architecture in Victoria open to the public. Fittingly, then, that this book describes the architecture and decor of Gyppeswyk. But it also describes the lives of the people who called it home: a fascinating and diverse group that included a banker, two lieutenant-governors, a department store magnate, and an artist-administrator—as well as their wives and children. The house may have begun its life as a private residence for well-to-do people, but today, as the heart of the Art Gallery of Greater Victoria, Gyppeswyk belongs to all the citizens of Victoria. We should cherish it.[3]

Easter Lilies by Sophie Pemberton, *c.* 1900: A watercolour of shooting stars and other wildflowers, which still grow in quiet corners of what was Alexander Green's estate. Once part of Sir James Douglas' Fairfield Farm, this land was described by the Hudson's Bay Company factor as "a perfect Eden."

THE HOUSE THE GREENS BUILT

Another Rocky Oak Place

Gyppeswyk was never intended to be a historical monument or a heritage treasure, much less an art gallery. Initially, it was the dream house of a middle-aged couple with six children. Alexander Green was a successful banker; Theophila Green was a busy homemaker. They had risked much to emigrate to a British colony on the west coast of North America but found Victoria to their liking—it was so much like the Old Country—and they wanted to establish themselves and their children in a comfortable, modern house that would also express their achievement and status. After living for several years in a small, uncomfortable bungalow, the Greens found just the spot to build a new home.

In 1843, the Hudson's Bay Company had established Fort Victoria. Impressed with several square kilometres of arable and pasture lands to the east of James Bay, James Douglas, chief factor of the fur-trading outpost and later governor of the colony of Vancouver Island, established a two-hundred-hectare estate he called Fairfield Farm. Along the northeastern edge of what was then quasi-prairie, the land slopes upward. This ridge is part of a rocky outcropping that runs north from Gonzales Hill, through today's neighbourhoods of Rockland and Fernwood,* to Smith's Hill, which is the site of the reservoir near

---

* In Fernwood, it's called "Spring Ridge" or "Fountain Ridge."

John O'Dreams by Sophie Pemberton, 1901: this oil painting, which now hangs in Gyppeswyk's foyer, is a scene that could have taken place on the mansion's grounds. When this picture was painted, Pemberton was still living with her widowed mother at Gonzales, the home her father Joseph Despard Pemberton had built at the corner of Rockland Avenue and St. Charles Street. A decade earlier, this pair could have been two of the Greens' children. Even if Pemberton did not actually know the Greens, she would have seen this sort of semi-rural landscape every day. ART GALLERY OF GREATER VICTORIA ARCHIVES 1954.010.001

the intersection of Cook and Finlayson Streets. Today, this rise of land is not so obvious, but travelling up the Fort Street Hill still challenges cyclists and low-powered vehicles.

An 1889 bird's-eye view of Victoria shows Gyppeswyk positioned atop this ridge but surrounded by largely vacant land—or rather semi-wild countryside. The northern boundary of this area, Cadboro Bay Road (later Fort Street), had begun to acquire a suburban look, as some wealthy Victorians had built homes along it in the 1860s and '70s. But to the south still sloped a Garry oak grassland or savannah, a part of Fairfield Farm with an idyllic, park-like appearance that reminded British settlers like the Greens of the rural scenes they had left behind. In this area of Victoria, they might hope to live on large estates, as they—or their betters—might have lived in villas or manor houses in the charming countryside back home. There was also a romantic hill sporting groves of oak trees, mossy stones, and spring wildflowers. In the fields below, a local Wordsworth might encounter not a "host of golden daffodils," but crowds of blue camas lilies. Such wildflowers, as well as purple shooting stars, or peacocks, and white fawn or trout lilies still grow on the northern part of what now forms the grounds of the Art Gallery of Greater Victoria. Even in the 1860s and '70s, the land east of Blanshard Street was still countryside. Writer Edgar Fawcett describes his schoolboy journey to Colonial School* at the top of the Fort Street Hill as a walk on a "pathway through the woods." A lake surrounded by willow and alder trees lay "on View Street, where there was good duck shooting in the winter."[1]

And, despite the rocky topography of this area, the drainage was good. Parts of Gyppeswyk are built on exposed volcanic rock, which forms a stony bluff obvious from Pentrelew Place but not so apparent when one approaches the house from Moss Street. Nearby Craigdarroch Castle has an appropriate name—it means "a rocky oak place"—and Rockland Avenue maintains a description of the area. Furthermore, from this rise of land, the views of the surrounding ocean, hills, and mountains were exhilarating to a generation of Britons who believed that beautiful vistas were both aesthetically and morally uplifting. This is probably why the Greens and their architect, William Ridgway Wilson, crowned Gyppeswyk with a rooftop belvedere, which still gives remarkable views in every direction.

Another reason for building a house on this hill was its elevation above the smoke, smells, and grime of nineteenth-century Victoria. This location, still partly wooded and exposed to the ocean breezes, was regarded as more healthful than a site down on Douglas or Government Streets. Near the heart of town, James Bay was a polluted inlet, giving off noxious odours. The many mills lining the harbour

---

* Now Central Middle School.

Gyppeswyk, *c.* 1950: The house in its last days as the home of the Spencer family. The porte-cochère has lost its railings. The large windows at the lower right mark the library. The curving driveway and the porte-cochère suggest both dignity and hospitality.

were also still burning soft coal and smoggy fogs were common in low-lying areas. As late as the 1950s, pea-soupers were occurring, in which visibility was limited to about three metres in front of one's car or bicycle. Perhaps our great-grandfathers realized that such smog was dangerous not only to traffic but also to personal health. And so, with this in mind—and because of the better views—Alexander and Theophila Green chose to build their dream home in Rockland and on the highest point of their new property, close to its northern boundary.

Rockland was also removed from the bustle and commerce of downtown Victoria. Although we may regard street scenes with horse-drawn carriages as quaintly picturesque, to many Victoria residents in the 1880s, the city seemed to be careening headlong into an unknown, dangerous future. Living in the countryside as landed gentry appeased their discomfort with social and economic change—however profitable it was and however much they benefitted from it! Which is why many a local entrepreneur and businessman aimed to live as a gentleman farmer.[2] This so-called Camelot Syndrome was a desire to return to a time perceived as simpler and less rushed than the present (an attitude not unknown in the twenty-first century). In interior decor, medieval times were idealized. At the intersection of Burdett and Linden Avenues, for example, the home of politician and businessman Richard Hall had a large wall mural depicting a scene from the legend of King Arthur and the Knights of the Round Table. A similar decorative theme is found in some of Gyppeswyk's decor. Nostalgia for a lost past is also evident in the Greens naming their house Gyppeswyk—a reference to the Old Country and typical of the wistful attitudes of transplanted Britons aspiring to be known as country gentlemen.

Contemporaries often called the Rockland area Government or Nob Hill, after the area settled by tycoons in San Francisco. Similar to their counterparts in California, Victoria's nouveaux riches had wealth and used it to indulge in conspicuous consumption. The Italian-style villas of the California rich inspired many homes in Victoria, including Fairfield House (now 601 Trutch Street), on the estate of Joseph Trutch, BC's first lieutenant-governor, and Judge Henry Crease's Pentrelew. In fact, for advice on additions to Pentrelew, Crease wrote to San Francisco architects Wright and Sanders. Pentrelew, whose name means "house-on-land-sloping-two-ways" in Cornish, was once a stone's throw from Gyppeswyk on Fort Street Hill, purchased in 1872 by Sir Henry Pering Pellew Crease (1823–1905), a British lawyer, judge, and politician. Crease had the Cambridge education and connections that placed him among the colonial elite. Perhaps to keep up with the neighbours, Pentrelew was enlarged in 1889, which is when the Creases would have seen the construction of Gyppeswyk.* Robert Dunsmuir, the local coal baron who built not

---

* Interestingly, in 1949, Pentrelew almost became Victoria's art gallery, which might have doomed Gyppeswyk to Pentrelew's ultimate fate: demolition.

a mansion but Craigdarroch *Castle*, would have understood Trutch's and Crease's motives. As for Alexander Green, his home was to be his monument, in the San Francisco style, but less dramatic and more practical than the residences of some of his neighbours. Whatever his motives—nostalgia, romanticism, escapism, or egotism—Green was a practical man. His rural estate was a five-minute walk from the new electric streetcar line running along Fort Street, which could carry him quickly to his Government Street office.

In any case, the building of Gyppeswyk was part of a trend. In the early 1880s, James Douglas' two-hundred-hectare (five hundred acres) Fairfield Farm was subdivided and became a district of smaller but still prestigious estates, some as large as 2.8 hectares (seven acres). This subdivision allowed Robert Dunsmuir to build Craigdarroch; David Williams Higgins, Regents Park (1501 Fort Street); Robert Ward, The Laurels (1249 Rockland Avenue); and Edward Gawler Prior, The Priory (729 Pemberton Road). All this mansion-building in the last quarter of the nineteenth century prompted an 1891 headline in the Victoria *Daily Colonist* exclaiming "Nearly Two Millions!" The associated article tallied up the cost of homes built in the previous year, especially in the Rockland area: ". . . it is doubtful if many streets in Canada contain a finer array of princely mansions than does Belcher Street [later known as Rockland Avenue]." It went on to note that Gisburn, at Rockland and Moss, had cost forty thousand dollars and that The Laurels had cost twenty-seven thousand dollars. Gyppeswyk was estimated to have cost thirty thousand dollars.[3]

Alexander Green's purchase was Lot 42, extending from the rear of Lot 3 on Fort at Moss down to Belcher. A one-storey log house with tiny windows stood on the property, but its original owner was unknown and it was immediately demolished. Until at least the 1930s, this property would retain the nature of a rural estate, with a meadow sloping gently downhill to Belcher Street. The Greens were relative latecomers to the Fort and Moss area. Almost thirty years earlier, the Bank of British Columbia had acquired from James Douglas

Gyppeswyk's west facade, 2011: Taken from Pentrelew Place. This is the more private part of the mansion, with the laundry wing and garage on the left and the Spencers' conservatory on the right. The bay window of the morning room is in the centre. The stone retaining wall, which was built when Pentrelew Place was put through in the 1930s, suggests the height of the land on which Gyppeswyk was built. The Garry oaks and rock outcroppings are still prominent.
PETER REID

2.24 hectares (5 acres) of land on the east side of Moss Street between Fort Street (or Cadboro Bay Road, as it was known then) and Rockland. Here, in 1867–68, the bank built Highwood, a large Italianate home, for its first manager, William Curtis Ward, brother of Robert Ward. It's address is now 1021 Gillespie Place. The following year, Judge John Hamilton Gray (1814–1889) of the BC Supreme Court and a Father of Confederation, erected a cottage he named "Homewood," on the southeast corner of Moss and Fort. In 1872, businessman Robert Burnaby employed architect Charles Verheyden to build a villa at the northeast corner of Moss and Fort. (The 1889 bird's-eye view shows all these structures.) Around 1890, Charles Rattray (or Rattrey) lived here. He was a clerk with Garesche Green & Co.—his boss, Alexander Green, lived almost next door. As well, a strip of houses lined the north side of Fort Street near the intersection with Moss. An elaborate wooden fence ran along Rockland Avenue, which was the southern edge of the Greens' estate, whose grounds consisted of about 2.4 hectares (6 acres) of gardens and orchards, with two tennis courts. A distance from the north side of the house (across what would become Wilspencer Place) was a coach house, a stable, and a paddock where the Greens' four horses and the children's pony could graze. Later residents the Spencers kept a cow on the property. A large lawn to the south was used for croquet and tennis. Although some of Rockland was given over to vegetable and dairy farms, much of the area was still almost wild. A young Frank William Green once shot a pheasant here, whereupon his neighbour, Judge Crease, sent him a summons and fined him twenty-five dollars![4]

Gyppswyk's architect, William Ridgway Wilson, as well as Alexander Green, and the home's later owner, David Spencer, probably recalled the great stately homes of the British Isles, with their vistas stretching away from their facades over greenswards, carefully maintained meadows familiar to twenty-first-century Canadians from British television serializations of classic nineteenth-century novels. Clearly, the Green property was a largely successful imitation of a British country manor for the landed gentry.[5]

In the early 1900s, suburbia began to encroach upon Gyppeswyk as areas to the east, west, and south of the mansion were subdivided. For example, the Craigdarroch Estate was divided up as Joan Crescent, Manor Road, and Craigdarroch Road were created. After the death of Gyppeswyk's last chatelaine, Emma Spencer, in 1934, the family began to sell off the extensive property where Alexander and Theophila Green had built their country manor. To the west, in approximately 1935, Pentrelew Place was developed and, by 1942, the land north of what became Wilspencer Place was sold, the Spencers having relinquished the property on which the outbuildings had stood. The land along the Rockland side of the estate was subsequently divided into lots and sold by 1943.[6] What had been originally a country retreat was becoming another suburban house, albeit a magnificent one. The reasons the Spencers began to divest themselves of the family property are not completely clear. However, the Great Depression, the Second World War, and competition (especially in Vancouver) had created new conditions for the Spencers' type of department store. And so divesting themselves of what had become useless property would have provided some added income, however briefly.[7]

A Villa in the Countryside

Although copies of the original plans for Gyppeswyk may lie in a dusty Victoria attic, or in some architect's forgotten filing cabinet, no plans or blueprints seem to be extant. Not until 1907 did Victoria require that structural plans and projected costs of new houses within city limits be filed at city hall. Consequently, some of what we know about the original layout of the mansion involves a degree of speculation. That said, Gyppeswyk obviously stands on a foundation of brick set upon rubble stone. Unlike Craigdarroch Castle (1890) or Hatley Castle (1908), it is a wooden frame structure with clapboard siding. At first, it was painted in earth tones of red, green, and light pink, colours that have been recently restored. (Similarly, down the street at Rockland and Moss, Robert Irving's Gisburn sported several colours on its exterior walls.) Although the exterior of the mansion may seem ornate, these muted colours make it blend in with its natural environment, which consists of green mossy rock outcroppings and the brown-grey trunks of oaks with dark green leaves. Later on, the Spencers painted Gyppeswyk white, giving it a more modern, if inappropriate, appearance (Ridgway Wilson and George Mesher— and probably the Greens—would have preferred that they stuck with earth tones).

Compared with the Dunsmuirs' massive structures, Gyppeswyk is relatively plain, with a symmetrical appearance on its eastern and southern facades that echoes the Eastlake-style decor of the foyer. Some elaborate wooden fretwork, however, decorates the eaves and

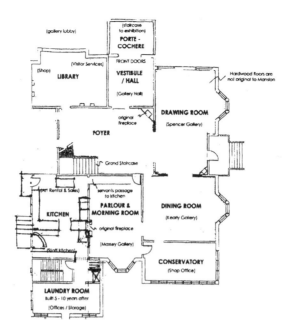

Main floor of Gyppeswyk, *c.* 1951 and 2012: Moss Street is at the top of the plan. Today, the library and the porte-cochère are gone. A glass-enclosed staircase serves as a fire escape on the north (Wilspencer Place) side of the mansion. The vestibule/hall included a cloakroom.

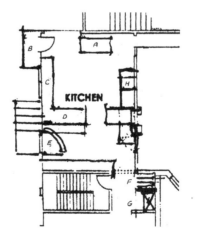

Plan of the kitchen, *c.* 1951: A large and sophisticated space, perhaps as laid out by Ridgway Wilson for the Greens but presumably how it was in the Spencers' time, and possibly also in the lieutenant-governors' time. A—stove; B—cold pantry; C—sink; D—cupboard; E—outside door; F—space for leaves of the dining room table; G—laundry chute; H—dumbwaiter.

brackets. Originally, a large elegant weather vane loomed above the belvedere. Extending from the east facade was the imposing porte-cochère. A conservatory ran along the east front of the main floor to the left of the entrance and extended a short way around the southeast corner of the house, where it was surmounted by a small turret. The Greens may have had an interest in horticulture, but maintaining an elegant greenhouse for plants also marked a family's wealth and status. Without adequate insulation and heating, this would have been a chilly place, although the sun's rays from the south and east may have improved the temperature within. We do not know how successful it was as a growing environment, but the Spencers had it removed during their residency. A door, covered porch, and stairway led from the south facade into the meadow. What we would today call an open veranda (or deck) flanked the porch on this side of the house. Another conservatory was added some time after 1906 to the west facade. On the north side was an enclosed porch, as well as a recessed portion that extended up two floors, with a coloured glass window in the centre.

Clearly, the look of Gyppeswyk's exterior changed over time. Around 1905, the Spencers built the so-called laundry wing and back stairwell, a two-storey addition at the northwest corner of the building. The upper floor is a glassed-in sunroom or solarium and may have contained a cistern for the storage of well water before running water was piped into the house. The room may also have later become another conservatory. Today, the concrete floor still slopes gently from the interior wall to the exterior one, presumably to catch runoff from the cistern or from the watering of plants grown there. Drains in the floor and traces of holes for pipes to bring water up to serve the cistern in the laundry room on the first floor can still be seen. The foundation of this wing is concrete. As already mentioned, a clothesline pulley is still attached to an oak tree on the northeast side of the building, evidence of the housekeeping that was carried on there when the Spencers, Grahams, and others made Gyppeswyk their home.* The line would have been connected to another reel on the porch of the laundry wing. As well, the Spencers added a garage at the northwest corner; its foundation is also modern concrete but its appearance, like that of the laundry wing, was designed to complement the style of the older building. (Its folding doors originally faced north but entry is now to the side.) Gyppeswyk was equipped with a chute that conveyed laundry from the second-floor gallery to the main floor. A dumbwaiter or lift, likely operated by hand, brought coal and kindling from the basement to the fireplaces on the upper floors; in the attic, there is a panel suggesting its original position. The up-to-date and wealthy Greens had enjoyed the use of a telephone (phone number 571) while living in their cottage on the southern extension of Government Street, an area called Birdcage Walk, and continued to do so later at Gyppeswyk (phone number 199).

The house's appearance is a mixture of Italianate and Queen Anne, which were popular styles in the late-nineteenth century. The Italianate parts of the house are the decorative brackets and the tall narrow windows, which include the Palladian windows on the south and east sides—each of which has a central, arched sash flanked by smaller rectangular sashes. The rooftop belvedere and the hipped roof, with surfaces that slope in four directions, also show the Italianate influence. The Queen Anne elements include the turret on the original conservatory, the projecting bay windows, and the elaborate chimneys.

If you had arrived at Gyppeswyk between the 1890s and the 1950s, your carriage (or your automobile) would have taken you up a curving driveway to the main entrance where a porte-cochère enclosed the front door of the house. There, you could pass from your vehicle to the interior of the mansion without encountering the elements. The flat roof of the porte-cochère was edged by an ornate wooden fence or railing, making it another vantage point for enjoying the fine views from the house. The original front door was a classical design, with

---

* The Greens, the Worlocks, and the lieutenant-governors likely sent out their laundry to one of Victoria's many Chinese establishments.

William Ridgway Wilson: Architect of Gyppeswyk, his name is often printed "Ridgeway"—even hyphenated as "Ridgeway-Wilson"—but his own signature drops both the hyphen and the "e" in Ridgway. Apart from being one of Victoria's most prolific architects, he had a military career just before and during the Great War (1914–1918), which this portrait suggests.

the typical triangular pediment supported by two pilasters. Coloured glass and tracery were used in the sidelights and in the transom above the door. The effect was simple but imposing.

The look of the foyer is sometimes referred to as Eastlake style, after Charles Eastlake (1835–1906), an English architect and writer, who encouraged the use of geometric ornament, incised lines, and relief carvings in wooden furniture and decor. This style was also used at Fairview, Robert Dunsmuir's first home in James Bay. Alexander Green, who initially settled in that area, would have known that house, or at least its exterior, and he may have sought to imitate it. Certainly Gyppeswyk's original appearance made a statement about modernity, luxury, and good taste.

The Architect: William Ridgway Wilson

As the architect for his mansion, Alexander Green chose a young man who, although not yet well-known or experienced, would go on to become one of the most prominent architects of his day in Victoria. Green may have identified with the twenty-six-year-old because he was another English immigrant. William Ridgway Wilson (1862–1957) was born to British parents in Hong Gow, China. His father was an East India merchant. At the age of thirteen, he was apprenticed to the firm of Bromitan Cheers in Liverpool before becoming an assistant in the London office of architects Searles and Hayes, and later working with Sir Horace Jones. Ridgway Wilson studied at the South Kensington Science and Art School and the Royal Academy before coming to Canada in 1887. By May 1888, he had formed a successful partnership with American-born Elmer H. Fisher (*c.* 1844–*c.* 1905) but after a year, the latter left to work in Seattle. He also briefly partnered with another English immigrant, Thomas C. Sorby (1836–1924), with whom he designed the Five Sisters Block in 1891, at the corner of Fort and Government Streets, named in honour of the daughters of Sir James Douglas. A modern structure, the building was heated by steam and lit by electricity.

At Gyppeswyk, *c.* 1951: The new curator of what had become Victoria Arts Centre, Colin Graham, and three young artists pose in the dining room, which Sara Spencer had used as a parlour. The Minton tiles on the fireplace were the only ones to survive the later conversion of the mansion into an art gallery but are now in storage.

Like his client, Alexander Green, Ridgway Wilson prospered in Victoria. In 1889, he married Flora Jenns, daughter of the rector of St. John's Anglican Church on Quadra Street, and together they had a daughter, Daisy (later known as Mrs. E.G. Mellander), and four sons, Guy, Hebden ("Dan"), Basil, and Percy. In 1898, the architect's home was at 60 Cook Street, but he moved with his family in 1899 to a house he had designed at 31 Gorge Road East, where they lived until 1927. Evidence of his professional success, this house, which has since been demolished, had stables and tennis courts. Later in life, he moved to 866 Craigflower Road.

Moving in influential upper middle class circles, Ridgway Wilson helped to found the Victoria Golf Club in 1893, serving on its rules and by-laws committee. He was also a member of the Empire Club and the Vancouver Island Arts and Crafts Society. (His wife, Flora, was a charter member of the latter club.) Ridgway Wilson knew Ray Worlock, Alexander Green's nephew, from when they both served with the 5th Regiment Canadian Artillery. During the First World War, the architect was a lieutenant-colonel in the Canadian Scottish Regiment (Princess Mary's) and commanded a prisoner-of-war camp in Vernon. (During that conflict, a partnership with Alexander Robert Hennell [1871–1961] carried on his architectural business.) Later, Ridgway Wilson became the Department of Public Works' district architect. He was also the architect for the BC Land and Investment Agency, which was founded by Englishman Thomas Dixon Galpin. (A portrait of Galpin's daughter Beatrice now hangs in the Kearley Gallery, Gyppeswyk's former dining room.)

In early life, Ridgway Wilson's health was delicate but he died at the great age of ninety-four. By that time, he had practised the longest continual architectural career in Victoria's history and counted among his clients some of the province's most noted celebrities. Martin Segger refers to the "dramatic fluidity . . . of his interior spaces," something that is very evident in the foyer and main rooms of Gyppeswyk.[8] Versatile and prolific, Ridgway Wilson designed many structures in Victoria—commercial, institutional, and domestic. His buildings include the Bay Street Armoury (now a national historic site), South Park School, and the Provincial Mental Home for the Criminally Insane (now the Wilkinson Road Penal Institution) in Saanich. In Gyppeswyk's neighbourhood, he also designed mansions like Shuhuum at 1322 Rockland Avenue (1894) and Prior House at 620 St. Charles Street (1911). At least one of his commercial structures, the Plimley auto showroom and repair shop at 1406–08 Pandora, is now a designated heritage structure, after having at one time served as the home of Victoria Arts Centre. In 1912, Ridgway Wilson

Fireplace in the foyer: The Minton tiles surrounding the grate show scenes from the legend of King Arthur; those on the floor represent the four seasons. The mirrors reflect the light and add a sense of depth to the space.

PETER REID

Part of the Victoria Brick Project opposite 1116 Government Street: A commemoration of the contractor, and sometime architect, who built Gyppeswyk according to William Ridgway Wilson's design. George Mesher left his mark throughout the city, with edifices such as the Yarrow and Sayward buildings and the October Mansions on Cook Street where David Spencer Junior and his wife lived for a while.

ROBERT RATCLIFFE TAYLOR

designed the extant W. & J. Wilson Clothiers premises at the corner of Government Street and Trounce Alley, which stands on the original site of Alexander Green and Francis Garesche's business. As well, he designed St. John's Anglican Church, which replaced the notorious "Iron Church."

The Contractor: George C. Mesher

On June 1, 1889, Ridgway Wilson called for tenders for the construction of a two-storey residence for the Greens on Moss Street and, two weeks later, George C. Mesher (1860–1938) was awarded the contract. Mesher had not formally trained as an architect but he had designed—as well as built—some important Victoria structures. Like Green and Ridgway Wilson, he was an English immigrant. Born in Weybourne, Surrey, Mesher learned contracting from his father (also called George). In 1886, with George Senior as his partner, he came to Victoria at the start of a building boom. In 1892, he returned to England to marry Janet Elizabeth McDonald. Their first home in Victoria was on Second Street, but they later lived on Dallas Road in a house Mesher designed in 1903.

The grand staircase in the foyer, 2011: The Eastlake woodwork on the newel post and balustrade, with its incised lines and geometric ornamentation, and on the panelled walls is largely intact today. In the 1970s, the foyer was fitted with couches and reading material for art gallery patrons. Washrooms were installed behind the grill. The chandelier originally in the dining room was once affixed to the newel post—upside down! (In 1999, its glass fixtures were repositioned when it was returned to its original site.)

PETER REID

The drawing room, *c.* 1952: Three patrons admire a painting above one of Gyppeswyk's distinctive fireplaces, still intact although the mansion was already the Victoria Arts Centre. The fire screen and hearth tools recall the recent use of this room for domestic purposes. Note the vivid Minton tiles. (Soon this fireplace and most of the other coal fireplaces, with their beautiful tiles and woodwork, would be removed.)
ART GALLERY OF GREATER VICTORIA ARCHIVES

The father-son partnership of George C. Mesher and Co. was one of the biggest contracting firms of the day in Victoria, their most important project likely being the Five Sisters Block on Government Street. Not far from Gyppeswyk, they built houses on St. Charles Street, Carberry Gardens, Linden Avenue, and Rockland Avenue. As in the case of the Sayward Building on Douglas Street, G.C. Mesher was occasionally defined as an architect.

The contract for Gyppeswyk was originally estimated to be "in the neighbourhood of $18,000,"[9] but some sources place the cost at $24,000, and the Victoria *Daily Colonist* claimed the final cost was $30,000.[10] To an extent, this increase may be due to the inevitable difference that exists (then as now) between the first estimate and the final construction cost of almost any building.

Generous, Hospitable Space

Although we have no photographs of Gyppeswyk's interior from when the Greens lived there, we can imagine a cluttered drawing room with high-backed chairs and cushions sewn by the ladies of the house, ornate lamps, a tea wagon, ornately framed photographs, and probably a piano. Heavy drapes flanking the windows were supposed to keep out "bad air," which it was believed could cause disease, such as "mal-aria." Appropriately, heavy green velvet tasselled drapes flank the bay window in the restored dining room (Kearley Gallery) today. Potted plants were also de rigueur. The Industrial Revolution had produced material goods for those who could afford them; hence, to display their newfound wealth, nouveaux riches like the Greens favoured generously upholstered furniture. Heavily patterned wallpaper was popular, as can still be seen today in the attic rooms, although whether this decor element dates from the Greens' or the Spencers' time is hard to determine. After the foyer, the dining room and the drawing room were the most important rooms in the house. There were no family rooms or rec rooms at this time.

Entering the house from the porte-cochère, you would have passed through a short hallway, with a cloakroom on the left, and then entered the foyer (or reception hall).[11] One of most impressive interior spaces in Victoria, it rises up two storeys and has a balcony (or gallery) lining the second floor. The style is Baronial, recalling manor houses in England, with the Jacobean-style ceiling coffered into grid-like compartments—as the Greens might have seen in Suffolk country houses.

In 1889, the interior decor of Gyppeswyk would have been considered the height of modernity and good taste. The foyer in particular met the ideal standards described by Clarence Cook, a nineteenth-century American critic and arts writer, whose work Ridgway Wilson and perhaps also George Mesher would have been familiar with. According to Cook, a reception hall "must be a large room, large at least in proportion to the size of the house." Space here should not

A ceramic hearth tile: Salvaged when Gyppeswyk's fireplaces were dismantled, one in a series showing scenes from Sir Walter Scott's novels. The artist was John Moyr Smith (1839–1912), a British designer and illustrator. Each tile functions like a still from a movie, capturing a dramatic moment in the tale. The literary reference was supposed to reflect the cultural sophistication of the mansion's owners.

ART GALLERY OF GREATER VICTORIA ARCHIVES SC 207

be "scrimped." Indeed, Gyppeswyk's foyer is exactly the "generous, hospitable space" that Cook recommended.[12] Here, as in the other main-floor rooms, a sense of spaciousness and light prevails, which contrasts with the small, relatively dark rooms of Craigdarroch. A large, coloured glass window in the then-popular art nouveau style, with floral/vegetable patterns, illuminates the foyer. Below the window is the grand staircase. As in other mansions and public buildings of the era, it is the focal point of the overall design, which gives a sense of possible pageantry and invites visitors to mount the steps. (Today, however, public access to the upper floors is prohibited.) The banister of this staircase is made of oak while the panelling of the foyer is cedar. With its simple geometrical shapes, the balustrade is ornate in the popular Eastlake style.[13] Craigdarroch Castle has a similarly small entrance hall leading to a highly decorated foyer and a staircase that extends up several storeys. As at Gyppeswyk, the ceiling is coffered, but the overall effect is not as light and airy—a feature that is much appreciated on Victoria's dark, rainy winter days. Even today, the polished sheen of the wood helps to brighten Gyppseswyk's foyer.[14]

A tall lamp graces the lower newel post of the staircase. Originally it was a gas lamp, matching the lighting elsewhere in the house. Holes in the walls of the foyer hint at where other gas fixtures might have once been installed. In Victoria, home electricity was available from 1884 onward, but the Greens' house was illuminated by gas, at least for the first few years of its existence.[15] The centrepiece of the foyer is an ornate fireplace with a wood mantelpiece and ceramic tiles. Such elaborate chimney pieces were intended to suggest their owners' wealth and were often designed to display bric-a-brac in small alcoves. This fireplace features ceramic tiles from Mintons Ltd., a major English ceramics manufacturing company founded by Thomas Minton (1765–1836), whose pottery factory was in Stoke-upon-Trent, Staffordshire, and which is today part of Royal Doulton Tableware Ltd. The tiles above the fireplace show scenes from the British legend of King Arthur and the Knights of the Round Table, while those on the floor reflect the four seasons, suggesting the agricultural pursuits of British gentry with manor houses in the countryside. Tiles with a pomegranate pattern flank the hearth, echoing the pattern of the dining room wallpaper. (Minton tiles were also used in Craigdarroch.) The Greens may have chosen the design from a catalogue or it may have been the architect or the contractor. Or perhaps the fireplace builders chose it, according to the taste of the time. In any event, as we have seen, people who imagined themselves as country gentry, like the Greens, tended to idealize the Middle Ages as a glamorous time, and the Knights of the Round Table had a patriotic cachet. In the hearth itself, the andiron (a metal stand used to hold logs or coal) features the heads of mythical creatures. Eleven other fireplaces, all coal-burning, were once part of Gyppeswyk. Today, the two other remaining originals can be seen in the morning room and upstairs

Stairs from the attic floor to the belvedere, 2011: Creaky, steep, and low-ceilinged, and much darker than in this flash photograph, they lead up to stunning panoramas of the city, the mountains, and the Strait of Juan de Fuca. They are virtually unchanged since 1889.
PETER REID

Part of the attic floor, 2011: The spot where the balusters of the concealed staircase for servants stood. From here, the help could move suitably unseen between the three floors of Gyppeswyk.
PETER REID

on the landing. The tiles of the latter have a variation on the Tudor rose, another reflection of Victoria's British heritage. Situated on its picturesque but windy hillside, Gyppeswyk must have been hard to heat effectively with only fireplaces and no insulation in the walls. The sliding pocket doors that seal off the drawing room from the dining room and the foyer were, therefore, probably heat-conserving and draft-reducing features. Originally, each room had a coal-burning fireplace, but they would have been small and could not have given off much warmth. The difficulty in heating such large spaces with only small hearths is reflected in the fact that a corner fireplace in the drawing room was a later addition made by the Spencers some time after 1906. The exposed radiator pipes in the dining room suggest that the Greens or the Spencers eventually installed central steam heating, which was available in Victoria by the 1890s. For much of Gyppeswyk's history, however, its inhabitants must have worn thick clothing.

Although several of the first British settlers in Victoria were well-educated men, by the 1880s the ownership of books, organized as symbolic capital in a library, was an indication of a gentleman's wealth, social status, and ostensible cultivation. Alexander Green certainly was wealthy, but it is hard to know if he actually enjoyed reading. In any case, the entrance to Gyppeswyk's library was a door on the east side of the foyer, to the right as you enter. As Mr. Green's and later Mr. Spencer's retreat, this room might also have served as a smoking room, to which gentlemen would have retreated after dinner with their port and cigars. In addition, if Alexander Green imagined himself a country gentleman, he might have used this room for keeping the accounts for his manor. No doubt it also later served lieutenant-governors as an office. A large, east-facing window allowed in plenty of natural light for deskwork, and a fireplace graced the north wall.

The smaller morning room was directly opposite the hall leading into the foyer. In most mansions, this room would usually face east to catch the warming rays of early sunshine. Gyppeswyk's faces west, but the views over the city would have been adequate compensation. While the servants made the beds upstairs and cleared away the remains of breakfast in the dining room, this room was where the chatelaines of the mansion would have retired to discuss meals with the cook, deal with correspondence, and briefly receive visitors. The room might also have been used as a breakfast room, and it was used as a dining room by the Spencers, who turned the dining room into their parlour. The morning room fireplace, with its ornate woodwork and tiles, is the second of the two still intact on the main floor of the house. The rosette in the ceiling is original but lacks its gas chandelier. The kitchen was reached through a door to the right of the fireplace. A small sliding (or pocket) door linked the morning room with the dining room. (Now covered over on the morning room side, this door can still be seen in the dining room.) Another door leads from the morning room into the conservatory, a later addition made by the

Spencers. The morning room is now called the Massey Gallery, after Governor General Vincent Massey (1952–1959), who presided over the opening ceremony for the art gallery (which was then called the Victoria Arts Centre).

The dining room of a modern home, wrote Clarence Cook, "ought to be a cheerful, bright-looking room," preferably with a southeast exposure.[16] Fittingly, Gyppeswyk's dining room, with its large bay window, looks out over the Japanese Garden to the south. Like much of the house, this room was illuminated by gas, lit by the large, gilded brass chandelier that still has the switches for turning the gas on and off. The plaster cornice and rosette in the ceiling are also original. The wallpaper had a floral/vegetable pattern, influenced by English designer William Morris (1834–1896) and the Arts and Crafts movement that stressed closeness to nature; similar wallpaper patterns were probably found in other rooms. The paper today is an 1864 Morris pattern of pomegranates, a style the Greens might have favoured. In the dining room, the walls at wainscotting level are covered with Lincrusta-Walton, an embossed linoleum product invented by Frederick Walton in Sunbury-on-Thames in 1877. For the Greens, this was a very modern touch. Servants coming from the kitchen could reach the dining room via a narrow passage between the morning room and the foyer. From this hallway, carrying trays of food and drink, they would pass through a small vestibule, then through the now-covered door into the dining room. This dining room was where part of the state banquet for the Duke and Duchess of Cornwall was held when they visited Victoria in 1901 as part of their tour of the British Empire. Given the large number of guests, the table probably extended into the drawing room. The long table usually found in this room today is one of the sort that would have been used for that great dinner. The larger pocket doors of the dining and drawing rooms could be opened up to create a single space, comprising the foyer, for entertaining, or could be closed for privacy or to conserve heat. In the Greens' time, carpeting covered the fir-planked floor of the dining room. (The present floor is not original.)

Northeast corner of the roof, 2011: Two of Gyppeswyk's elegant chimneys, now capped and repointed. They express the verticality of the Italianate style.
ROBERT RATCLIFFE TAYLOR

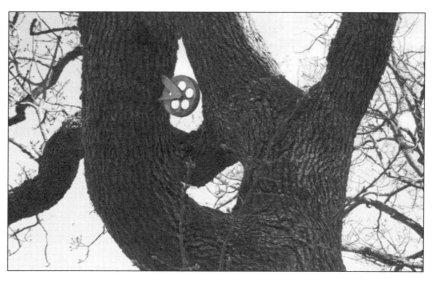

Relic of a clothesline at the rear of Gyppeswyk, 2011: A pulley still affixed to one of the Garry oaks at the rear of the mansion is a reminder that Gyppeswyk was always home to couples and children with the usual domestic needs.
ROBERT RATCLIFFE TAYLOR

The parquet-floored drawing room acted as a living room, or a room for receiving guests, but takes its name in part from the practice of guests dividing by gender following a formal meal, with the men staying in the dining room (or going into the library) to converse, drink, and smoke, and the ladies *withdrawing* to a different room. Again, Clarence Cook's idea of perfect modern interior design is exemplified: "So far as possible, all the rooms in this ideal home front the sun, or are visited by the sun for an hour or two every day."[17] Two large windows flank the main fireplace and another bay window admits the sun for certainly more than the recommended hours each day.

Gyppeswyk has eighteen rooms in all; eight of them are bedrooms on the second floor. Most of these rooms face east, south, or west, guaranteeing them plenty of the required natural light. The master suite was on the east side and included a bedroom and an adjoining sitting room. Here, Alexander and Theophila Green—and later David and Emma Spencer—could have retreated from family, community, and business responsibilities. From most of the upstairs windows, they could have seen the Strait of Juan de Fuca and the Olympic Mountains. And in the spring, they could have admired blue carpets of camas lilies and the enclosed meadows where sheep and cows from the other local estates grazed. On the second floor, most of the rooms are interconnected, perhaps to facilitate ease of movement and private communication in an era when servants might have been prowling the halls. A large linen closet, now the photocopy room, was reached by a door on the west side of the landing. The current staff washroom on the south side of the house is probably the original bathroom.

Whether or not Gyppeswyk was originally supplied with running water or connected to a city sewer is not clear. By the 1880s, however, the provision of running water in modern homes was increasingly considered necessary. By 1881, the chief factor's wife, Lady Douglas, had running water in her home. Flush toilets were also being installed in wealthier homes, the first self-acting water closets having been installed in Victoria in 1877. Craigdarroch and Pentrelew had water closets by 1890. When it was built in 1894, Ridgway Wilson's South Park School had flush toilets and drinking fountains. By comparison, despite its elegance and modernity, when it was completed in 1889, Gyppeswyk would not have had reliable running water from civic water mains, nor a hookup to the sewage system. So, for a few years at least, the Greens must have relied on a well on the premises.

By 1890, water mains had been installed along Fort Street to the Jubilee Hospital and along Rockland Avenue to Government House. As well, fire hydrants had been installed at the northeast corner of Fort and Moss Streets and at the southwest corner of Rockland Avenue and Moss Street. Presumably around this time, household water service was available along Moss Street between Fort and Rockland, but Gyppeswyk likely had to wait until 1909 and the construction of the concrete water tower on Laurel Lane for a totally reliable supply of water. As for sewage, Gyppeswyk's residents probably used a septic tank until 1892, when sewer mains were installed on Moss Street.

Gyppeswyk's third floor—really a glorified attic—has four oddly shaped rooms wherein lived the servants. A narrow, twisting staircase connected these quarters with the second floor. The holes where the newel and spindle posts of this staircase once rested can still be seen in the floor, and a narrow door from the hallway leading to the laundry wing marks the access to these stairs. The Greens certainly did not want the help bustling up and down the main staircase in an unseemly fashion. And so, typically, the movements of this essential labour force were hidden away in such small corridors or behind concealed doors.[18] The west-facing attic room has a round (or bull's-eye) window; the east- and south-facing rooms have Palladian windows.[19] There is no trace of fireplaces or radiators in the servants' rooms on this floor, so we have to assume they were unheated. They would have been warm enough in the summer, but very cold in the winter. The belvedere was—and still is—reached by another narrow staircase from the attic. The prospect of magnificent views may explain the sloping structure that connects to one of the belvedere's walls beneath a window: artists may have used it.

A gloomy partial basement eventually housed the coal furnace, and the remains of the coal chute can still be seen, as can the immense rock outcroppings upon which Gyppeswyk is built. The basement had at least one room with a window that offered accommodation for a live-in janitor, but the rest of the floor is just a shallow crawlspace.

Photographs of the gardens that originally surrounded the house are few, but even after Gyppeswyk's owners sold off the estate-like grounds that slope down to Rockland Avenue, the mansion remained surrounded by lawns and shrubbery, firmly "under the oaks." A rose garden and a rockery fronted the south facade (the site of the present Japanese Garden), and the tennis courts lay between there and Moss Street (where the Pollard Gallery stands today). By this time, the curving driveway had been surfaced with concrete, the mansion set back impressively from Moss Street and framed clearly through the trees.

This was the house that Alexander and Theophila Green had commissioned, suitable for the size of their family and commensurate with their perceived importance and social position. Its construction was noted by the *Colonist* as an important city event. Architect William Ridgway Wilson, the newspaper wrote, "has completed plans for a handsome residence" that "will be one of the largest and handsomest in Victoria."[20] When the Greens relocated from their cramped quarters on Birdcage Walk in 1889, they must have been delighted with their new, modern, and imposing home. They would also have been pleased with their social progress. The trajectory of their lives had taken them half a world away from Suffolk to the most elegant and socially prominent neighbourhood in Victoria, a city that had evolved dramatically from the rugged gold rush boom town that had mushroomed up on Vancouver Island shortly before their arrival in 1873.

Yates Street, *c.* 1860: Looking west from Government Street. This was the outpost of Empire that David Spencer and Alexander Green found when they arrived from Britain. The buildings on the left suggest the modern city that was emerging from the gold rush boom town. The street, however, was still redolent of the pioneer days, with a drainage ditch running down its centre.

THE FOUNDING FAMILY

Gold Fever

Although Gyppeswyk was not built until 1889, the reason for its existence is found in the Fraser River Gold Rush—and its impact in the
decades that followed. So we must ask, what sort of community did
Gyppeswyk's first owner, Alexander Green, and its later owner, David
Spencer, find when they arrived in Victoria in the 1860s and 1870s?[1]

Little Fort Victoria, founded by the Hudson's Bay Company in
1843, was a sleepy place. Even by 1858, only about two hundred people
lived within or near its palisades. Beyond the fort, local residents were
connected in some way to the HBC, which operated fairly prosperous
farms, but a few settlers managed independent establishments. The
small community had three schools, a doctor, and a clergyman with
one church. In the early 1850s, however, some changes began taking
place. By 1856, a legislature had been founded and elections had been
held. The British naval base at Esquimalt was developing. Lumber
was already being exported, and the booming economy of the future
was foretold by the discovery of coal at Nanaimo. But the pace of life
was slow and the fort continued to be isolated in the far west. The
Canadian Pacific Railway had yet to be built, the Panama Canal did
not yet exist, and the journey by sea around Cape Horn took months.
A profound jolt came when gold was discovered on the Fraser River
in 1858.[2] Overnight, the formerly quiet community became a staging

post where would-be miners stocked up on necessities before heading up the Fraser River and later to Rock Creek, Wild Horse Creek, Big Bend, and the Cariboo. When David Spencer arrived in 1863, there were already around six thousand people living in Victoria. Most of these gold-seekers expected to be transients, but many, like Spencer, became permanent residents. Businesses thrived and fortunes were made—not on the riverbanks of the BC interior, but on Government and Fort Streets. Inevitably, the possibility of instant wealth from gold finds gradually diminished and, so, many newcomers settled down in Victoria to seek their livelihood from the infrastructure that the gold rushes had created, or, increasingly, from coal mining or lumbering.

Arriving in Victoria in 1873, Alexander Green actually missed the hurly-burly of the city's gold rush days. That same year, David Spencer, who had arrived earlier, was already busy founding the first of his dry-goods stores. Green may have appreciated the fact that the boom town was now a more sedate community offering stable business opportunities. Nevertheless, photographs of Victoria's downtown in the 1860s and '70s still show a relatively rugged-looking place. Even on Government Street, board sidewalks and false fronts characterized many of the buildings. On windy days, clouds of dust rose from the unpaved streets; in rainy weather, citizens could sink ankle-deep in mud. Alexander Green, of course, had made his fortune in the wilds of Australia and had seen the raw exuberance of pioneer Nevada, not to mention the Yankee bustle of San Francisco. These inconveniences, therefore, would not have troubled him much.

Outside of Victoria's mud and dust lay beautiful scenes reminiscent of England. As already mentioned, the climate and geography of southern Vancouver Island was, in fact, appealing to British settlers, especially those who loved romantic landscapes. Arriving in Victoria in 1859, Henry Crease, a lawyer, judge, and later Fort Street neighbour of the Greens, described the "balmy air & lovely scenery—soft tho' so rocky & wild. (It's awful rocky & woody everywhere)."[3] In fact, although the Greens set up house on Birdcage Walk, they eventually purchased a summer home on Gonzales Bay overlooking the Strait—a place with balmy air and lovely scenery—before building Gyppeswyk. With its predominantly English ruling class and temperate climate, Victoria may have seemed a little like Suffolk, where Alexander Green had grown up.

However, the decade during which David Spencer and Alexander Green arrived in Victoria was also one of unsettling changes for the city, and many locals had to adjust their lifestyles and their horizons. An economic depression set in around 1865. The Vancouver Island colony was subsequently absorbed by mainland British Columbia in 1866, and by Confederation with the rest of Canada in 1871. Nevertheless, the community was starting to look less like a frontier outpost. By 1873, the remaining buildings of the old fort had been demolished. By that time, too, Victoria had been incorporated as a city, and had been the provincial capital of British Columbia since 1867. Furthermore, the streets were beginning to look modern in certain ways. Alexander Green, the businessman, would have appreciated the large stone and brick warehouses lining Wharf Street. Several hotels had been built and were, according to a British visitor, "elegantly furnished [and] . . . supplied with every comfort and luxury." As well, he noted, a theatre seating four hundred was "sometimes visited by able and respectable dramatic troupes."[4] Gas street lighting had been introduced and some stores were lit with gas. Modern businesses had been established on Government Street, which is where Alexander Green found employment and where David Spencer had already set up shop. Fire engines were in service and some streets had even been macadamized. Two newspapers supplied the news and seven churches offered spiritual sustenance. In fact, when newcomers such as Spencer and Green arrived (in 1863 and 1873, respectively), Victoria was already in the midst of taking on characteristics that would mark it for decades.

Victoria was—and is—an unusual city, partly because of a geographical location that has inspired generations of poets and artists, and partly because of its inhabitants' relatively high degree of literacy and appreciation of the arts. Compared to other pioneer communities in western Canada at that time, the city was sophisticated; Victoria was not the wild west. As Michael Kluckner has pointed out, even before 1858, the rugged fur-trading outpost looked "different" from other contemporary settlements, characterized by "rambling farms and estates in the English tradition."[5] Although London's plan to stock the colony with men of upper-class birth and education was never fully successful, a considerable degree of what contemporaries called "refinement" and "culture" prevailed.

The Hudson's Bay Company officials as well as later immigrants from Britain definitely exhibited a high level of literacy. Appointees to government positions in Victoria were selected partly on the basis of their educational achievements, and degrees from Oxford or Cambridge were favoured. A review of commercial establishments shows that nineteenth-century Victoria residents enjoyed reading, which would have included novels, drama, and poetry. In 1858, Thomas Hibben established a stationery and bookstore. In 1864, David Spencer purchased J. Corin's reading room and bookstore. Other early Victoria residents had large personal libraries, such as Benjamin William Pearse, assistant to the Surveyor-General of Vancouver Island, J.D. Pemberton. By the 1880s, Victoria also had a Shakespeare Club and the Alexandra Club for the enjoyment of music, art, and literature. The Worlocks (who lived briefly at Gyppeswyk in the 1890s) and especially the Spencers enjoyed and participated in musical performances.

From the city's beginnings, education was important to Victoria citizens. On the outskirts of the city, Craigflower School, considered the first Canadian school built west of the Great Lakes, was founded in 1854. In the 1860s, a girls' collegiate school was founded by the Anglican authorities. In 1865, a board of education was established, along with the beginnings of a public school system. Like many other well-to-do English immigrants, Alexander and Theophila Green wanted to send their children to schools in England, but David and Emma Spencer, who could have afforded to send their offspring to the Old Country, saw their children suitably educated in Victoria.

By the 1860s, due to the gold-seeking outsiders inundating Victoria, the colony had been transformed from a "quiet English village" to a "busy commercial centre."[6] Many firms had moved north from San Francisco, American ships were making regular stops, and one US enterprise had founded a newspaper, the *Victoria Gazette*. The well-known American company Wells Fargo Express had opened a Victoria location in 1858, at the start of the gold rush. At first, Colonel C.C. Pendergast and Major James Gillingham operated the branch, which was then located on Wharf Street. In 1866, Francis Garesche (later Alexander Green's partner) became its local agent, advertising his role as a "Dealer in Exchange, Bullion and Agent for Wells Fargo Express . . ." Mail was brought in regularly from San Francisco and handled by Wells Fargo's Yates Street office, which later moved to the southwest corner of Government Street and Trounce Alley. The office was thronged with men waiting for parcels and even letters on days when the steamer arrived.

Commercially and culturally, therefore, Victoria was the most advanced settlement of the British western Pacific. But while the city attracted people from the United States, French Canada, Europe, and Hawaii, and had a large Chinese population—some of whom would live and serve at Gyppeswyk—Victoria's governing and cultural elite still hailed mainly from England, which may have been why Alexander and Theophila felt at home.

Alexander Alfred Green: Respected Citizen

Alexander Alfred Green (or A.A. Green, as he usually identified himself for business purposes) was born in England in 1833 in Ixworth, Suffolk. His father, William, and his grandfather were medical doctors. Young Alexander Alfred attended the Woodbridge grammar school and is said to have studied medicine with his father.

He may also have been apprenticed to an apothecary. Around 1860, at the age of twenty-seven, he sailed from Britain to Australia in search of gold. Described as "a youth with a brilliant flair for answering when opportunity knocked,"[7] he made a fortune in the Antipodes, and then went on to Nevada and California, where he joined Wells Fargo. How long he spent in California is unknown, but, in the later nineteenth century, Victoria was a relatively short step away from San Francisco, linked more closely by geography and communication to that city than to the rest of Canada. The two coastal communities also shared some similarities. White settlements had begun in both places in peaceful isolation, only to be suddenly transformed by a gold rush. When offered a post in Victoria, Alexander Green would have seen the similarities as well as the important difference: Victoria was British. After leaving California, he seems to have visited Victoria briefly, then travelled to England, where he married Theophila Rainer, before eventually settling in Victoria with his bride.

But why did Green originally leave home, parents, friends, and familiar surroundings for an uncertain future? Perhaps he believed that he had somehow failed to meet his father's expectations in medical study. While some young men have an inherent yen for adventure—particularly adventure that might make them rich—Green may have also believed that Britain's financial crash of 1858 restricted opportunities for advancement at home. Moreover, in the latter half of the nineteenth century, the social privileges of middle- and upper-class Englishmen were being challenged politically and economically. Furthermore, the British Medical Act of 1858 raised standards and demanded increased discipline in the medical profession; higher qualifications and more demanding examinations may have daunted young Alexander. The expansion of scientific knowledge also made the practice of medicine more complicated. Unlike in the past, all these factors would have militated against a young man seeking a secure financial future as a medical doctor.

Alexander Alfred Green: Photographed in his prime by the accomplished Victoria photographer Hannah Maynard, probably around 1880. His beard, moustache, and hat suggest his younger adventurous days in Australia, Nevada, and California; however, by this time, he was one of Victoria's leading citizens and a successful banker. (Another photo taken at the same time shows him to be bald.) Gyppeswyk was a tangible symbol of his professional and social success.

Theophila Rainer Green: Alexander Green's wife, also photographed by Maynard, widowed by his death in 1891, after which she struggled to keep his business afloat and maintain Gyppeswyk as her home.

Alexander Green could be described as typical of many in his generation. Henry Crease also considered trying his luck in the goldfields of Australia. And three years after Green first left England, David Spencer left Wales in the same pursuit of gold and perhaps also with the same sense that Britain's economy had no hope of satisfying his ambitions. Of course, Spencer was Welsh and of the yeoman class, both of which would have limited his social mobility. In any event, Alexander Green, with his wife and baby daughter, arrived in Victoria as a representative of Wells Fargo in late 1873, and his previous work experience won him a position as an accountant with Francis Garesche in the Victoria branch of Wells Fargo, which would eventually become part of the services of Garesche Green &·Co., a private bank.

Founded in 1852, Wells Fargo Express employed the stagecoaches that became iconic symbols of the American West. As we have seen, the business had expanded to Victoria by 1860. The company established its local banking service in 1866. Born in Wilmington, Delaware, in 1829, Francis Garesche, the Wells Fargo agent for Victoria, had, like Alexander Green, made his way to California in 1855. He was married to Clara Teresa Malet of San Francisco and was probably Roman Catholic. The couple lived at 633 Michigan Street, not far from the first homes of the Greens and the Spencers. At one point in his career, Garesche was elected to the local board of education.

Alexander Green used the fortune he had accumulated in Australia and Nevada to build (or maybe purchase) a house in the most attractive and fashionable residential neighbourhood of the city, James Bay, which was also home to Garesche, David Spencer (and later two of his sons), Emily Carr's family, and, of course, Sir James Douglas. In 1874, the Greens lived in a one-storey bungalow with a veranda at 15 Birdcage Walk, just east of the Birdcages, the first Legislative Buildings of British Columbia.[8] (The Spencer family lived just across the street at the corner of Belleville and Birdcage Walk.) The house, which the Greens called Ferndale, sported wrought-iron decorative birdcages, replicas of the ones in Kensington Gardens in London.[9]

Emily Carr grew up a few blocks away from Ferndale and was best friends with Edna, the Greens' eldest daughter, for many years. Carr describes life at Ferndale in the 1870s:

Two of the Greens' sons: Ray, who like his father became a prominent banker, is on the left; Frank William, later a well-known physician and MLA, is on the right. (No contemporary portrait of the youngest son, John Bertram, a surveyor, is extant.)

The Greens were important people. Mr. Green was a banker.
They had a lot of children so they had to build more and more
pieces on to their house. The Greens had everything—
a rocking horse, real hair on their dolls, and doll buggies,
a summer house and a croquet set. They had a Christmas tree
party every year and everyone got a present.[10]

Originally, this part of James Bay must have seemed pleasantly removed from the business heart of Victoria on Government Street, but over time the stench rising from the tidal flats-cum-garbage dump that was the bay might have made their choice of residence seem less salubrious.

In any case, the Greens lived at Ferndale until 1889. When plans for the new Legislative Buildings were being developed, they took the opportunity to build Gyppeswyk. In leaving the once-fashionable James Bay area, they were part of a trend: the Worlocks and the Spencers, among others, eventually forsook James Bay for the more spacious lots, better views, and healthier air of Rockland. As for Ferndale, after Alexander Green's death in 1891, Garesche Green & Co. used it as a residence for employees until it was sold in 1893.

"A Meteoric Business Career"[11]

Alexander Green was a typical nineteenth-century self-made man. He obtained his wealth and relatively high social position not because of any connection to the Hudson's Bay Company or the Royal Navy, nor because he was in a profession needed by the colonial government. He did, however, qualify as a gentleman, an advantage that David Spencer did not have. Despite this leg up, Green could be said to have succeeded on his wits alone. Once settled in Victoria, with the fortune that he had amassed in Australia and the United States, he achieved a social position that would have probably been impossible for a man even of his bourgeois background in class-ridden Britain. His new Moss Street home and its extensive

The Greens' daughters: Left to right: Edna, baby Dorothy, and Mary Amelia. (A fourth daughter, Gladys, died in infancy. Her small tombstone can be seen next to the Greens' monument in Ross Bay Cemetery.)

property reflect his achieved social status, which was almost the equivalent of a country squire or gentleman farmer on a large estate in the Old Country. As on such properties elsewhere, Green's estate had stables and a paddock for horses. (Nearby, Joseph Despard Pemberton bred horses and cattle.)

The Green family was conscious and proud of having achieved a social eminence they could not have attained back in Suffolk or

The Green family, *c.* 1895: The six surviving Green children group around their widowed mother. Left to right: Frank William, John Bertram (standing), Dorothy (seated), Theophila, Edna (standing), Ray, and Mary Amelia (standing).

HP 054706 C-07299, COURTESY OF ROYAL BC MUSEUM, BC ARCHIVES

Norfolk. This is illustrated by the size and opulence of the family's monument in Ross Bay Cemetery. A large, gleaming, red marble pedestal dominates the Green family plot, which stands directly on one of the major carriageways, making a statement to any passersby.

Certainly, by the time of his death in 1891, banker Alexander Green had become, as his obituary observed, "a respected citizen."[12] He was what his contemporaries called a progressive, "go-ahead" businessman. By 1880, for example, he was one of the directors of the Victoria and Esquimalt Telephone Company, which established the city's first telephone connections. He was said to have enjoyed "popularity" and to have possessed a "positive integrity,"[13] which no doubt enabled Garesche Green & Co. to prosper. He may also have indulged in land speculation because he applied to buy one hundred acres at Bamfield Creek in 1882, and was co-owner of several hundred acres of the Nicola coalfields near Merritt.

Gravesite of the Greens at Victoria's Ross Bay Cemetery: The last resting place of Alexander and Theophila, and several of their children and grandchildren. As well, Kate Pegram (1875–1968) is buried here. (She may have been a niece of sisters Theophila Green and Martha Worlock. A third sister, possibly Mary Ann Rainer, married a Mr. Pearce and lived in Vancouver. Their daughter, Kate Pearce, married William Henry Pegram in 1893.)

ROBERT RATCLIFFE TAYLOR

Soon after his arrival in Victoria, Green joined the first congregation of the Reformed Episcopal Church, which was within walking distance of Ferndale. He was elected a warden of that church, which was known later simply as the Church of Our Lord. Throughout the 1870s, Green served as people's warden and was active on the church committee. In 1887, he served on the local committee organizing the celebrations for Queen Victoria's golden jubilee. He was also on the directing committee of the British Columbia Benevolent Society and was a director of the new Royal Jubilee Hospital. As well, Green was co-manager of the bequest of John George Taylor (an Irish immigrant also affected by gold fever), who had set up a fund for the welfare of the city's children. In this capacity, Green was, for a time, president of the board of directors of the Protestant Orphans' Home (now the Cridge Centre for the Family) near the corner of Cook Street and Hillside Avenue, where he would possibly have crossed paths with David Spencer, who served on the board of management.[14] Green was also a Freemason.

Alexander Green must have hoped to live another ten or even twenty years beyond his allotted "three score years and ten" in what later generations would call his dream house. But, after suffering for several years from "an internal cancer,"[15] he died in 1891 at the age of fifty-eight. His funeral was an important local event that year. Pallbearers included Mayor John Grant and publisher D.W. Higgins, as well as Gyppeswyk's architect, William Ridgway Wilson. Between three and four hundred friends and acquaintances personally called on his widow at the mansion to express their condolences. The funeral was "of more than ordinarily impressive character," according to the *Colonist*, reflecting the opinion that Alexander Green was "a kind and sympathetic friend and a public and philanthropic citizen." At Gyppeswyk, possibly in the foyer, "the body was enclosed in a massive cork [open] casket, highly polished, with gold and silver mountings, which soon became partially hidden in the wealth of flowers which filled the house with perfume."[16] Such verbiage and

Ferndale, the Greens' house on Birdcage Walk: Mrs. Green, Mrs. Cridge, and the seven Green children. Bishop Cridge, and his wife and family, lived a few blocks to the south. The Spencers lived across the street. Alexander's business was a fifteen-minute walk across the James Bay Bridge and up Government Street.

HP 005710 B-02178, COURTESY OF ROYAL BC MUSEUM, BC ARCHIVES

ornate trappings exemplify the typical nineteenth-century culture of grieving, but they also contain a sense that Green was indeed a respected and admired person.[17] Attending the Ross Bay Cemetery interment were, among others, his three sons and the younger members of the Garesche family, as well as "the gentlemen of Garesche Green & Co.," who included his wife's brother-in-law Frederick Worlock and his nephew Montague Raymond Worlock, plus John Barstow Chantrell and John Coltart, who were both clerks at the bank.[18]

In his management of his bank and in his personal economy, Green may have made some unwise decisions. However, several external factors may also have contributed to the failure of his banking business in 1894. A local real estate boom collapsed, and a smallpox epidemic raged in 1892. As well, the depression in the 1890s would have affected

Garesche Green & Co. no matter how sound Alexander Green's practices were. Business had slumped in the United States, where banks were closing regularly, the price of wheat was falling steadily, and the Colorado mines had slowed production. Inevitably, British Columbia was affected and unemployment grew. The question of how Green—had he lived—would have handled these challenges is open to debate. His illness and demise may themselves have contributed to the failure of his business. For even near bankruptcy, a living Green might have rallied, gone on to some other endeavour, and prospered. He might even have enjoyed the success of his contemporary David Spencer, who would move into Gyppeswyk in 1903, having enjoyed almost phenomenal business success. (Spencer lived to the grand age of eighty, passing on a thriving business to his sons, who would administer it for another quarter-century.)

Garesche Green & Co.

Especially in the aftermath of the various gold rushes, Francis Garesche, and later Green, too, did a thriving business in gold dust and selling bank drafts to miners. In October 1875, shortly after Green had joined Francis Garesche at Wells Fargo Express, the business moved from Yates Street to Government Street, opposite the post office, at the corner of Trounce Alley.[19]

Unfortunately, Garesche did not work at this new location for long. As we admire the floating palaces—those cruise ships that dock at Ogden Point—and relish the by-now-traditional sailing of the MV *Coho* to and from the Inner Harbour, it is easy to forget that the waters around Vancouver Island and Washington State can be treacherous. In the late nineteenth century, the sinking of passenger vessels was not unusual. In November 1875, Francis Garesche set off for San Francisco, accompanying a large Wells Fargo shipment of gold dust. His ship, the *Pacific*, sank off Cape Flattery. His body was never recovered.

For Green, however, this tragedy was a blessing in disguise. In 1877, while continuing to control part of her late husband's business

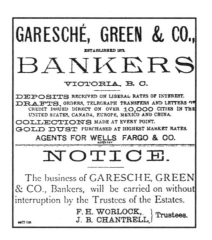

Garesche Green & Co., 1891: A version of the company's advertisement that ran for several years. Alexander Green had just passed away and the lower section had been added to assure clients of the bank's continued operation.
VICTORIA *DAILY COLONIST*, OCTOBER 17, 1891.

interest, widow Clara Garesche admitted Green as a partner in the business, which became known as Garesche Green & Co., Private Bankers and Agents for Wells Fargo. The enterprise became a private bank, and began serving the Allen Shipping Line of England. The Garesches' son George Henry worked for the company as a teller until 1892. With Alexander Green as manager and holding a controlling interest, the business flourished. Although not a chartered bank, it issued letters of credit and handled bills of exchange, and claimed to have connections to cities in Canada, the United States, Europe, Mexico, and China. By 1892, the firm was advertised as "the largest private banking house in the Dominion . . . [with] . . . capital equal to that of many of the chartered banks of Eastern Canada."[20]

In fact, around this time, the business seems to have outgrown its premises. In 1889, while still building Gyppeswyk, Green commissioned Thomas Trounce to design what would became known as the Green Block, a two-storey brick Italianate building that still stands at the corner of Broad Street and Trounce Alley, directly behind Garesche Green & Co.'s bank. The Green Block was originally twinned with another structure on the south side of Trounce Alley.

The Green Block, corner of Broad Street and Trounce Alley, 2010: Originally in exposed brick, probably dull red in colour, it is now known as the Exchange Building. It was twinned with another identical building to the south, which was destroyed in the 1910 fire.
ROBERT RATCLIFFE TAYLOR

Alexander Green's plans in 1891: Sixty feet fronting Government Street and 240 feet running along Trounce Alley, this building would have housed his expanding business. Its imposing four stories would have made a dramatic statement of his success on Government Street.

ELLIS & CO., "VICTORIA ILLUSTRATED." *THE DAILY COLONIST*, 1891

In August 1889, the stables on the site of the north structure were torn down, after which contractors Elford and Smith began building the twin structures. They ran one hundred and twenty feet down the alley, each with fifty feet of frontage on Broad Street.[21] The remaining Green Block (1210–1212 Broad Street) sports a large dome above the second floor at the corner, with two smaller domes on the Broad Street side and many little turreted domes on the Trounce Alley side. (Its identical twin across the alley to the south burned in the 1910 fire that devastated central Victoria.)

Green rented out space in the Green Block to the Victoria and Esquimalt Telephone Company, in which he had an interest, and to the Young Men's Christian Association, both on the second floor, where the latter stayed until approximately 1909. (The YMCA had previously been located in Spencer's Arcade just to the south of Government Street.) Other businesses, including a bicycle dealer and an insurance agency, also rented space in the building. From 1928 to 1930, the Victoria Stock Exchange was housed there, so the building is still known as the Exchange Building. In 1995, it was restored by architect John Keay.

In 1891, the year he died, Green was still envisaging expansion. He planned to build a three-storey structure on the business' location at the corner of Government Street and Trounce Alley that would have extended back to the northernmost edge of his recently completed buildings on Broad Street. It would have been the new, imposing location of Garesche Green & Co., and would have made a dramatic statement on Government Street. Needless to say, this structure was never built.

Immediately after her husband's death, Theophila Green announced that his business would "be carried on without interruption."[22] The appointed trustees were Frederick Worlock, formerly assistant manager of the firm (and her brother-in-law), and John Barstow Chantrell, a clerk with the company. In 1892, Mrs. Green became sole owner of the business when she purchased the share held by the Garesche estate. She then appointed Worlock general manager and admitted him as a partner. The brief history of Green Worlock & Co. was troubled, but when it collapsed in 1894, the entreprise had enjoyed a long and prosperous history, and was probably the last private bank to operate in British Columbia.

Theophila Turner Rainer Green

Alexander Green's wife, Theophila,[23] was born to John Smith Jackson Rainer and his wife, of Great Yarmouth, Norfolk, in 1840. Her early life was marked by two tragedies. In December 1863, she married Frederick Bird in Ipswich, Suffolk. Her young husband, with whom she had no children, died there in 1867. Theophila married Alexander Green in June 1872. (Witnesses were her father and Alexander's father, William Green). A year later, she gave birth to twins, a girl and a boy. The girl, Edna Theophila, survived but the boy was stillborn. Undaunted, she immigrated with her husband and baby to Britain's remote colonial outpost on the Pacific coast of North America.[24]

Like many women of the time, Theophila was courageous in making such a move into the unknown, especially with a young child whose robustness might have been questionable. She probably had an independent frame of mind, too, for she usually identified herself by all her family names: Theophila Turner Rainer Green.

One of Theophila's younger siblings, Martha Amelia Rainer, married Frederick Hammett Worlock in Ipswich in September 1873. In the nineteenth century, family members typically assisted each other when immigrating to Canada—as they still do. The Rainer sisters were no exception, probably missing their former intimacy with each other. In 1888, the Worlocks came to Victoria and Frederick found work in Alexander Green's business.[25]

In 1892, the widowed Theophila Green went back to England to visit her family whom she had not seen for over twenty years and to enroll her younger children in schools there. Despite the precarious nature of travel, especially before the opening of the Panama Canal in 1913, such a return visit to the Old Country was not unusual for Victoria's wealthy class. Among Victoria's well-to-do, the trip to Britain was often deemed necessary in order to enroll their children in socially approved schools, and later to check up on them. All the Crease children, for example, were sent to Britain to complete their education, or to learn about their English background and visit relatives. And we know James Douglas visited his daughter in school in England in 1874. Moreover, for many Victoria people, having travelled in the British Isles and Europe was a mark of social and cultural sophistication.[26] Theophila, therefore, felt the need to give her younger children the advantage of an English education.

Back in Victoria by 1894, Theophila continued to make Gyppeswyk a centre of social and cultural activity despite the failure of her late husband's business and her approval of the decision by the trustees of the Green-Worlock Estate, Gyppeswyk's legal owners, to put the house on the market. In December 1896, for example, a "merry company" of "the ladies of the Reformed Episcopal Church" had "one of their periodical conversaziones" there, with "plenty of song and stir."[27] The trustees had put Gyppeswyk up for sale in 1895, around the same time the Greens' summer house on Shoal Bay went on the market, but the former did not sell, partly because of the lingering effects of the depression that ended the era of massive mansion-building (at least for a while). Eventually, in 1899, the trustees leased Gyppeswyk to the provincial government as a residence for the lieutenant-governor, making it a source of revenue for the estate's debts. At this time, Theophila moved to a residence on Fairfield Road. With four of her six children independent and/or married, whether she decided to move out of the large Moss Street mansion or was encouraged to do so by the trustees, we cannot know. In any event, she soon moved from Fairfield to a two-storey house she had built at 1 Stanley Avenue, at the corner of Fort Street. She lived there with her youngest son, John Bertram, and her daughter Ada Dorothy. As the owners of four other properties, on Yates and View Streets, the household was still prosperous enough to employ a cook named Chung. Theophila died in 1905 in Victoria and is buried with her husband in Ross Bay Cemetery.

The Green Children

As was customary in the nineteenth century, Alexander and Theophila Green had a large family. They may have been late starters who had one "frost blossom" but the Greens eventually conceived eight children, six of whom survived to adulthood (one baby died at birth, another in infancy). At the time of his death in 1891, Alexander's three sons and three daughters were all still living at Gyppeswyk.

In 1892, Ray Green (1876–1930)—also known as Alexander Rainer—was a clerk with his late father's business, Garesche Green & Co. He then spent a few months at school in England. When he returned to Victoria in 1895, he identified himself as a teacher, perhaps because when the family business failed, he was either out of work or doubted his prospects in banking. However, he remained interested in his father's profession as a career. By 1898, he had moved to Vancouver, was living on Bute Street, and was working as a bank clerk (or ledger-keeper) with the Imperial Bank on Comox Street. In 1906, he married Babette Ethel Wolfe. By 1913, he had become the branch manager of the Imperial Bank on Denman Street. By 1915, he was back in Victoria, managing the Imperial Bank at Yates and Government Streets—a position he held until his death—and living on Victoria Avenue in Oak Bay.

It appears that Ray Green committed suicide in the South Thompson River in 1930. On a train trip from Vancouver to Toronto, he got off the train in Kamloops at around eleven o'clock at night and, leaving his hat and coat on a coffer dam bridge, "entered the water." He was only fifty-four years old at the time but had been "in indifferent health for some time." Just three years younger than his father when the latter died, it is possible Ray had inherited the same "internal cancer" that killed his father. Ray was described as "a man of sterling character and genial disposition" with "a host of friends."[28]

His younger brother Frank William Green (1877–1953) attended John Wesley Church's Corrig College, an English-style "public school" for boys, located at the corner of Niagara and Douglas Streets. He did not live at Gyppeswyk for very long because at some point after his father died, he left Victoria to study medicine at McGill University, fulfilling his father's original career plan. He had some of his father's adventurousness, too. Upon graduating as a physician in 1898 at age twenty-two, he became the Canadian Pacific Railway doctor at Goat River Crossing on the Crows Nest Pass line in the Kootenay Valley. He served the line on horseback and operated a forty-bed cabin hospital, where he treated many men during a typhoid epidemic, burying the dead himself in a cemetery near the hospital. In 1899, he set up practice in Cranbrook with another doctor. His son also became a doctor and they shared a practice in the early 1950s. Frank Green also served as the Conservative–Coalition MLA for Cranbrook from 1941 to 1949. He was "a kindly man who didn't say much," wrote James Nesbitt, "but when he did he packed considerable wallop."[29] He died in Cranbrook in 1953.

John Bertram Green (1880–1967), the youngest son, also had a successful career. When his mother's plan to enroll him in school in England failed, he attended Corrig College with his brother Frank. Like his other brother, Ray, he tried his hand at banking, starting as a clerk with the Bank of British Columbia in 1899. By 1901, he had become a clerk for the wealthy businessman Robert Ward (who lived not far from Gyppeswyk on Rockland Avenue). In 1904, John Bertram moved to the Bank of Commerce on Government Street, where he shared an office with poet Robert Service, who later became famous for his poem "The Spell of the Yukon." In old age, John Bertram maintained that when their employer had a job opening in the Yukon, it was offered first to him but he turned it down. Service, the bank's second choice, accepted the position.[30] (If Service's young colleague had accepted the job, the history of Canadian poetry might have been different.)

At this time, John Bertram was still living on Stanley Avenue with his mother and sister. By 1905, he had become a professional land surveyor in British Columbia. For decades, he worked out of an office on Station Street in Duncan, operating mainly in Cowichan and southern Vancouver Island. Having once shot a pheasant, he still enjoyed hunting: there is a photograph, circa 1900, of him standing on the shore of Cowichan Lake with a bear he had shot. In 1909, in Quamichan, he married Agnes (or Ann) Robertson, with whom he had three children. They lived on Tzouhalem Road. After Agnes' death in the 1940s, John Bertram married Isobel Ainslie Hall. He died in Victoria in 1967.

The three Green boys inherited their father's intelligence and abilities. At Corrig College, they often received high marks on their exams and were skilled football players.

The Greens' daughters had the education middle-class parents in Victoria considered suitable for their female offspring. They learned domestic skills from Theophila, while their governess provided them with more formal education. At least two of them attended a private school as day pupils, where they would have learned to improve their reading and writing skills, and to appreciate literature, art, and music.

Edna Theophila Green (1873–1953) was the eldest child, born in England just before the Greens immigrated to Canada. As a child and teenager, she was the best friend of Emily Carr, who was a frequent guest at the Greens' homes on Birdcage Walk and Moss Street. In the late 1890s, she taught kindergarten in the former home of Francis Garesche at 933 Michigan Street, another example of how few degrees of separation existed at the time in Victoria. (And at the time the house was owned by George C. Shaw.) Respectable young women of the time whose financial situation had become precarious or who had no father or husband to support them often found that the only socially acceptable profession was teaching, especially in the subject of music. Her sister Ada Dorothy did the same thing after she and her mother moved to Stanley Avenue. However, Edna and Ada may not have been desperate financially—it may just have been that, like their mother, they had an independent cast of mind and wanted some freedom and work satisfaction before they married.

In any case, in 1901, Edna married Edward A. Carew Gibson who worked for the Department of Agriculture and later as a manager with Granite Quarries in Vancouver. She died in Coquitlam in 1963. Both she and Edward are buried in the family plot at Ross Bay.

Mary Amelia Green (known as Millie) was born in 1878. She won a scholarship for theory and piano offered by the Misses Wey in 1896. (The Wey sisters, Annita and Lillian, lived just down Moss Street from Gyppeswyk.) Not much more is known about Millie, except that she eventually married David D. McLaws of Winnipeg.

When graduating in 1896 from Clovelly College on Rockland Avenue, Ada (or Anna) Dorothy Green (1881–1940)—known by her second name—distinguished herself by winning prizes for "scripture" and for having the highest marks in geography, English, and Canadian history. She also studied music with the Misses Wey and performed at recitals, causing a local journalist to note that she would "make a good pianist."[31] She became a teacher, opening a kindergarten and primary school at Gyppeswyk in the fall of 1897. Later, when living with her mother on Stanley Avenue, she operated the Victoria Girls' School as principal (with a Miss Dawson). This was a boarding and day school that advertised "Kindergarten, Primary and Advanced Classes."[32] In 1904, she was associated with the Royal Alexandra College of Music and Art. She married Charles Norman Barclay in 1908.

In 1887, Gladys Julia (or June) Green died at the age of fourteen months of bronchitis, for which there was no cure at the time. A small, white marble headstone at the Green burial plot is almost illegible but the word "Baby" can been deciphered.

The 1891 census recorded that Gyppeswyk was home to two "Chinamen," one sixteen years old, the houseboy, the other twenty-five, the cook. These servants probably also cleaned the house and maintained the gardens. People like the Greens often preferred Chinese servants to those of British descent because the latter might work for only a few weeks before getting married and moving on. These Chinamen were probably two of the many, in Emily Carr's words, "raw, neat pig-tailed China boys" who often arrived from Asia at the tender age of twelve.[33] Many of Victoria's mansions had a "Chinaman's room" in the basement, attic, or near the kitchen, although some of these servants would have returned to Chinatown at night. At Gyppeswyk, these two servants could have lived in a room in the basement or in the attic.

As already mentioned, the Greens also had a summer home on the northeastern slope of Gonzales Hill that overlooked McNeill (Shoal) Bay. Part of what would become Oak Bay, the area was cottage country for Victoria citizens in the nineteenth century. Here, they retreated on summer Sundays to enjoy what were still relatively wild surroundings and a beach frequented by native people with canoes. John Bertram remembered being fascinated by these people. He also remembered being thwacked on the head by an older brother—and having the wound treated by pioneer physician John Sebastian Helmcken, a friend of the family from their days on Birdcage Walk.[34]

Wealthy businessmen of the nineteenth century often groomed their sons to take over their enterprises. Robert Dunsmuir did so, and Alexander Green may have intended to do so as well. The oldest son, Ray, did enter his father's business but when it collapsed, he had to seek employment in Vancouver, although still in banking. John Bertram, the youngest, seems also to have wanted to pursue a career in banking. He could not join the defunct family firm, but did enter the banking world—with the Bank of Commerce. However, he soon gave it up for other work. Therefore, unlike in the family of

David Spencer, no commercial dynasty developed among Alexander Green's children.

In 1894, when Theophila and her children returned from England, Gyppeswyk briefly became home to two related families. With three adults and ten children resident, the mansion must have been bursting at the seams.

The Worlock family: Left to right: Montague (Ray), Martha, Winnifred, Frederick (who took over the late Alexander Green's business), Katharine, and Ethel Mary. Close relatives of the Greens, the two families shared Gyppeswyk for several years.

JUST VISITING

On May 21, 1893, the *Colonist* noted that "the musical Society enjoyed their 'closing evening' of the season last week, at Gyppeswyk, the home of Mr. F.H. Worlock"; the programme was "impromptu" and the performers received a "hearty vote of thanks."[1] The mansion now had new residents: Frederick and Martha Worlock and their four children, music lovers all. After her husband's death, Theophila Green had travelled back to England and had stayed for two years. During this time, she seems to have thought it both prudent and considerate to invite her sister Martha and Martha's husband, Frederick, along with their family, to live at Gyppeswyk. After all, Frederick had been assistant general manager of Garesche Green & Co. and was her brother-in-law. He had also become her business partner and knew the business well. Moreover, in its owner's absence, a large, expensive mansion should not remain vacant for long.

When Theophila returned from England, she and her children shared Gyppeswyk with the Worlocks. So from 1892, the Worlocks lived with the widow Green ("Aunt Green" to her nieces and nephew) and several of her children, a sensible arrangement for both security and sentimental reasons.[2] In 1895, Theophila seems to have wanted to sell the mansion, perhaps because several of her children were growing up and—the boys at least—were almost ready to be self-supporting. At this time, the estate's trustees objected because legally the children could have an interest in the house. In the end, Theophila remained in nominal possession of Gyppeswyk until 1899.

Frederick Hammett Worlock

Frederick Worlock, who became a familiar figure in Victoria, was born in Bedminster, England, in 1848. He married Martha Amelia Rainer (Theophila's sister) in Ipswich in September 1873. All of their children were born in England. For a short time after emigrating in 1886, the Worlocks lived in Winnipeg, where Frederick worked for Wells Fargo. They moved to Victoria, apparently upon the invitation of the Greens, so Frederick could work in his brother-in-law's business. Soon after their arrival in 1888, he was employed as a clerk with Garesche Green & Co. and the family was living on Princess Street. By 1891, the Worlocks had moved to Rae Street (now Courtney Street, between Douglas and Quadra). They moved into Gyppeswyk some time in 1892. After living in Gyppeswyk for about two years, Frederick and his family returned to their peripatetic lifestyle. In 1895, they moved to Rockland Avenue, then to Vancouver Street, to Pemberton Road, and finally to Menzies Street in 1902, where they lived until at least 1905.

Frederick's professional life was varied as well, and gold fever and Wells Fargo played roles in it, as they did for his late brother-in-law. After the failure of Green Worlock & Co., Frederick remained the local agent for Wells Fargo for a while, and then, as the Klondike Gold Rush took off, he worked for the Canadian Development Company in Dawson City as "General Commission Agent" (or manager) for Taylor, Worlock & Co. Ltd., which represented Wells Fargo. However, this firm seems to have been short-lived. His health compelled him to return to Victoria in 1904, where he worked in the salmon canning industry, and later was superintendant of the Victoria-Phoenix Brewery from 1908 to at least 1925. During that period, he and his wife lived on Rithet Street. When he died in 1926, he was once again living on Menzies Street (this time at #16). Obviously, Frederick's professional life did not have the clear trajectory of Alexander Green's and certainly not that of David Spencer's so perhaps he was actually less astute than descriptions of him suggest. However, he was certainly what his contemporaries would have considered dedicated to commercial progress and his own financial success.

On the east side of Rockland Avenue, Frederick owned the second house in from Oak Bay Avenue, popularly called Worlock Cottage, which he rented to the province in 1893 as a temporary home for Lieutenant-Governor Edgar Dewdney (1835–1916) while repairs were made to Cary Castle. (Interestingly, six years later, a fire at Cary Castle would force his successor, Lieutenant-Governor Thomas McInnes, to move into Gyppeswyk.)

Known as a "kindly and benign presence," Frederick was, like his brother-in-law, active in the community. He was involved with the Rotary Club and the Canadian Club, and served on the board of the Protestant Orphans' Home. He was also an accomplished amateur musician, occasionally singing solos in concert—as in April 1891 at the Reformed Episcopal Church—and was one of the original members of the Arion Male Voice Choir. "He took a deep interest in music," said his obituary, "and was possessed of an excellent voice."[3] In addition, he played cricket, serving in 1892 as president of the Albion Cricket Club. When he took over the management of Alexander Green's business, Frederick was described as a "gentleman of large experience in banking, of great energy, of exceptional courtesy and . . . highly esteemed as a banker and a citizen."[4]

Green Worlock & Co.

Unfortunately, Frederick Worlock's personal qualities, if attributed accurately, do not seem to have helped him and Theophila Green avoid financial disaster at 81 Government Street. By 1894, the company was faced with possible bankruptcy and, on March 2 of that year, it did not open its doors for business. Frederick announced that the closure was only temporary but the doors never re-opened. Even as late as 1926, a Vancouver journalist would note that the "disastrous failure" of Green Worlock & Co. "created [a] sensation."[5]

The immediate cause of the bank's demise was the failure of Wells Fargo to honour a draft for a large sum, a default that may have resulted from the recession afflicting North American and European economies from January 1893 and June 1894, and causing business activity in Canada and the United States to stagnate. Possibly Alexander Green's investment in a large, expensive mansion as well as in new business premises had strained his personal finances as well as the bank's. Of course, his death removed the man under whose direction the business had flourished and under whom it might have survived, even in difficult times. Misdirected family loyalty may have also been a cause of the company's demise. Alexander—and Theophila too—seems to have trusted Frederick Worlock to manage the business, a potentially unwise move.

In any case, despite having a reputation for "financial strength, fair dealing and sagacious methods" for more than twenty-five years,[6] the Green and Worlock bank failed. Its books were said to be "in a lamentable condition" and its assets "practically worthless."[7] Soon afterwards, there are references simply to the "Green, Worlock Estate." In 1894, Theophila and Frederick assigned their real and personal property to the trustees of Alexander Green's estate. The trustees were Frederick, then former company clerk John Barstow Chantrell, and later (after Frederick withdrew) John Coltart, the company's former principal accountant; Henry Frederick Heisterman, a Victoria real estate agent; and James Stuart Yates, a barrister. Eventually, Coltart and Heisterman were replaced by Robert Beaven (1836–1920), a businessman who also served as premier of BC and mayor of Victoria. As these men dealt with the estate's problems, they were empowered to advance regular payments from the estate to Theophila and her children.

At the time of its bankruptcy, Green Worlock & Co. had been facing a "steady reduction in deposits" but, with Frederick as its spokesperson, promised "all claims would be satisfied in full." Frederick pleaded with creditors not to launch legal proceedings against the firm[8] but many immediately did, and by 1895, one of the Green buildings on Broad Street was up for sale. In 1898, however, Theophila and Frederick were still listed as the building's owners.

"Puzzling legal questions"[9] about the company's procedures subsequently erupted, and there was much wrangling among the creditors over its future. For example, at one point, Beaven claimed that local chartered banks would not render the private company any assistance. This assertion was denied by Frederick, who also disagreed with the other trustees over the true state of the bank. At another point in the proceedings, the creditors insisted that Coltart and Heisterman be replaced as trustees partly because they felt Coltart's position as principal accountant with the firm rendered his judgement unreliable. Moreover, they believed that the trustees' plan to take as long as four years to settle the firm's debts was much too long. This led to Beaven replacing Heisterman, but the tangled affairs of the Green Worlock estate were not cleared up until at least 1908.

Faced with the loss of their savings, many private individuals and local store owners expressed "consternation and surprise" when Green Worlock & Co., which had been "considered a substantial financial institution," collapsed.[10] Ultimately, only one chartered bank received what it had claimed from Green Worlock & Co., while ordinary depositors and other creditors were paid only a small amount of their claims. However, the company's fate was not unique. Between 1867 and 1914, the failure rate of Canadian banks, 36 per cent, was even higher than that of US banks. Twenty-six banks failed in Canada during this period, and in nineteen cases criminal charges were laid.[11] That no criminal proceedings were launched against Frederick Worlock suggests that the business had been honestly—though perhaps not efficiently—operated but still could not withstand the violent economic storms of the early 1890s.

Martha Rainer Worlock

Martha Amelia (or Angela) Rainer was born in 1852 and married to Frederick Worlock in 1873. She came to Victoria in 1888 with her husband and four children. She became an active member of the Women's Auxiliary of Christ Church Cathedral and of the Royal Jubilee Hospital, and was also active in the Bishop Cridge chapter of the Imperial Order of the Daughters of the Empire. Martha worked with the Ladies' Committee of the Protestant Orphans' Home, donating clothing to the orphanage and, in 1893, offering raspberry jam. (We have no record of whether or not she made the jam herself or if the berries were grown on the grounds at Gyppeswyk.) She was especially active socially and charitably throughout the 1890s.

The Worlocks enjoyed a more active social life than the Greens. For some reason, although not as prosperous as their relations, the Worlocks were more successful in penetrating the highest social circles. Loving music as much as her husband and children did, Martha seems to have enjoyed dancing, for she and Frederick attended several balls while living at Gyppeswyk. For example, in November 1893, she and Fredrick attended the Jubilee Hospital Ball, during which, with Dr. George L. Milne, MLA, she led one of the "sets of honor in the opening Lancers."[12] (No evidence exists, however, of any dances having taken place at the mansion during their time there.)

While living once again on the still fashionable Menzies Street from 1902 to 1904, Martha and her husband retained a sixteen-year-old male servant, Ah Nun, a Buddhist. Perhaps he had moved with them to Gyppeswyk, but there is no record of any servants' names from that time. (Conceivably, any of Gyppeswyk's Chinese servants could have remained there after Alexander Green's death and until 1899, when Theophila and her children moved out.) In 1905, when her husband's professional ambitions took him to the Yukon, Martha was living (presumably alone) on Dallas Road. After being widowed, she moved back to Menzies Street where she lived until about 1930. She died in Victoria in 1940.

The Worlock Children

Frederick and Martha Worlock had a son, Montague Rainer Clifton, and three daughters, Ethel Mary, Winnifred, and Katharine. Like the Green children, and the Spencers, they loved music. Whereas most well-bred (though not necessarily talented) young ladies and gentlemen of the time took music lessons, Frederick Worlock and his children seem to have been genuinely gifted amateur musicians, and were deeply involved in concert-giving at their temporary home of Gyppeswyk and elsewhere in the city.

Montague Rainer Clifton Worlock was born in 1879 in Barton Regis, Gloucestershire. "Ray" (as he liked to be known) was a teenager when his parents and sisters moved into Gyppeswyk in 1892. He distinguished himself as a tenor, singing the anthem during evensong at Christ Church Cathedral on at least one occasion. He was also a member of the Arion Male Voice choir from 1898 to 1905 and served as secretary from 1900 to 1902. Like his father, uncle, and cousin Ray Green, Ray Worlock pursued a career in business. By 1895, he was working with his father at Wells Fargo, which survived the bankrupt Green Worlock & Co. In 1899, he worked for Turner Beeton & Co.'s clothing factory. Soon Ray was employed as a clerk with the Molsons Bank. Changing employers, he worked from 1901 to 1904 at the Imperial Bank on Government Street, as had his cousin. In his spare time, Ray was enrolled with the 5th Regiment Canadian Artillery, 1895–1902. On the regiment's cricket team, he was a very good bowler, and in 1900, he served as acting sergeant in the absence of Sergeant William Ridgway Wilson, Gyppeswyk's architect. In 1905, Ray married Beatrice Mary Lucas in Seattle and moved to California where he worked as an auditor until, although living in Piedmont, he enlisted at Victoria in September 1917. Ray and his wife lived in Prince Rupert in 1926, but spent the later part of their lives residing on Roslyn Road in Oak Bay. Ray died in Saanich in 1957.

Ethel Mary Worlock was born in 1875, when her parents were still living in Ipswich. A talented girl, she won a prize for "general proficiency" at Spring Ridge School when she was fourteen. At the prize-giving, she gave a recitation. In an 1891 public concert, Ethel played a piano quartet with three other girls. At another concert, in 1899, she gave two contralto solos. Ethel had been appointed a teacher at North Ward School in 1896, and was living with her parents on Vancouver Street. In 1904, she married Captain Charles Slingsby Fall of the South African Constabulary in Capetown.

Winifred Worlock was born in Bristol in 1878. She seems to have been less talented than her older sister, although she did attend the Misses Wey's School in the company of Millie Green and the Misses Heisterman. She married William Holmes in 1897.

Katharine Worlock, the youngest daughter, was born in 1880, in Barton Regis, Gloucestershire. She attended Miss Kitton's Victoria College, where she won a prize for "scripture" in 1893. She married Edmond Hale Austin of Quebec in 1903.

As for Gyppeswyk, after the Greens vacated it in 1899, it did not languish empty for long, but became what many considered BC's most outstanding residence and home of the monarch's representative: Government House.

THE LIEUTENANT-GOVERNORS

A public announcement on May 25, 1899, stated that the "Green residence" had been rented from the Green Worlock Estate for fifty dollars a month as the new residence of British Columbia's lieutenant-governor. The two men who subsequently lived at Gyppeswyk as vice-regents could not have been more different in their backgrounds, personalities, or conduct. The tenure of the first was a failure; that of the second, a resounding success. They and their chatelaines brought contrasting lifestyles to the Moss Street house.

A Gentleman of More than Ordinary Ability

In 1899, after a decade as a private home, Gyppeswyk became a public building when Thomas Robert McInnes (1840–1904) took up residence there. The vice-regent was born and raised at Lake Ainslie on Cape Breton Island, the son of John McInnes of Inverness, Scotland. On the occasion of his swearing in as lieutenant-governor of British Columbia, the *Colonist* described him as "a gentleman of more than ordinary ability . . . a conscientious man."[1] Indeed, McInnes had already had several careers and had succeeded at most of them—until he became lieutenant-governor. After teacher training in Truro, he studied at Harvard. He then attended medical school, after which he served in the Union Army during the American Civil War. Back in Canada, he was successful as a doctor

77

Lieutenant-Governor Thomas Robert McInnes: In the uniform he saved from the 1899 fire at Cary Castle. Although he and his family lived at Gyppeswyk for only a short time, this testy vice-regent left his mark on British Columbia's constitutional history.

and was, at one point, elected reeve of Dresden, Ontario. By the 1870s, McInnes was at Royal Columbian Hospital in New Westminster, BC, and served as mayor from 1876 to 1877. In 1881, he was made a senator. A Presbyterian, he described himself variously as senator, barrister, and physician.

In 1890, McInnes moved to Victoria, where he lived at 110 Michigan Avenue in James Bay, not far from the Worlocks. He and his wife, Martha, had a relatively luxurious home that had previously been the manse for St. Andrew's Presbyterian Church. It was fitted with walnut, oak, and mahogany fixtures imported from England and included fine china, glass, rugs, and paintings. A large garden was notable for its ten-foot-high hedge of holly.

Prime Minister Wilfrid Laurier appointed McInnes lieutenant-governor in 1897. Confusion surrounded this appointment because, when Ottawa publicly announced his new role, he had not yet been sworn in and so insisted on claiming that he was not yet lieutenant-governor. This stubborn punctiliousness marked his tenure in British Columbia.

In 1898, McInnes enjoyed the distinction of opening (with a gold key) the provincial legislature in the new buildings designed by Francis Rattenbury. His term in office, however, was marked by disaster and controversy. The famous fire of May 1899 that destroyed Cary Castle, then the lieutenant-governor's official residence, wiped out all the McInneses' personal possessions, valued at three thousand dollars. One morning on his way to breakfast, the lieutenant-governor's private secretary, his son Tom, heard a crackling noise, and alerted the rest of the home's inhabitants to the fire he discovered in the upper storey. McInnes himself had to "run the gauntlet of falling embers,"[2] managing to save only his official uniform. Firemen had to restrain Martha from re-entering the house to retrieve her jewels. A defective flue was said to be the source of the conflagration. The house was an almost total loss, which necessitated the move to Gyppeswyk.

Martha McInnes: Her introspective pose expresses the attitude of a devoted wife and mother. She was unaccustomed to the pomp and circumstance required in the life of a vice-regent's partner.

Two years before this calamity, Thomas and Martha McInnes cannot have totally welcomed the move from their commodious Menzies Street house to Cary Castle, described by a local journalist as "picturesque, dignified, and drafty."[3] Perhaps the McInneses hoped that Gyppeswyk would be a permanent replacement for the eccentric Cary Castle, as it was more modern and less quirky in appearance and layout. But any house built on the Cary Castle property would have a more commanding position than Gyppeswyk, with better views of the Strait of Juan de Fuca and the Olympic Mountains. Moreover, a Government House on that elevated site could also be seen from a distance, at least from the south, establishing the vice-regal presence.

The McInneses do not seem to have entertained much either at Cary Castle or at Gyppeswyk.[4] McInnes may have been too overwhelmed with his political predicaments or may simply not have been as sociable as some other lieutenant-governors. In any event, toasts offered at dinners held at Cary Castle and Gyppeswyk had to be with non-alcoholic beverages because even wine was forbidden by the teetotalling vice-regent. It is thus doubtful that during this period the mansion would have seen many gentlemen retreating to the library for port and cigars.

On the other hand, McInnes continued the practice of hosting New Year's Day levees, as inaugurated by Lieutenant-Governor Trutch in 1872. On the first day of the year, people from many different walks of life trooped into Gyppeswyk to shake McInnes' hand. We can imagine them admiring the beauty of the grounds and the woodwork of the foyer, then still new and modern.

Quiet and retiring, McInnes' wife was not comfortable at large social or fashionable occasions. Martha Webster was born in Maine. She was the widow of George Webster of Dresden, Ontario, when she married McInnes in 1866. She offered little in the way of entertainment at Government House, in either of its locations—although she must have appreciated Gyppeswyk's comparatively large, light-filled

Tom M[a]cInnes: After his brief stay at Gyppeswyk, the lieutenant-governor's eldest son went on to become one of the most prolific Canadian poets of his generation. His books of poems have evocative titles, such as *In Amber Lands*.
FRONTISPIECE TO *IN AMBER LANDS*, 1910

rooms. Not inclined to be sociable, she showed little interest in the wives or families of the local elite, which probably did not help McInnes' popularity as vice-regent. However, she had two sons with Thomas—William Wallace Burns and Thomas Robert Edward—to whom she was devoted. Martha died in 1929 at the age of one hundred and one.

No record exists of how many servants the McInneses brought with them to Gyppeswyk, but we may assume that they had the usual retinue. At Cary Castle, Lieutenant-Governor Hugh Nelson had employed five servants from 1887 to 1892, including two Chinese. McInnes' successor, Henri Joly de Lotbinière, as we shall see, employed five servants when he lived on Moss Street in the 1900s.

A Ruritanian Comedy

Using these words, Professor S.W. Jackman described the political conflict that marked McInnes' term in office.[5] In fairness to the lieutenant-governor, it was not entirely his fault. The political situation in BC was, to say the least, unsettled. Party loyalties and discipline did not yet exist so that, in the legislature, combinations and alliances were often shifting. Nevertheless, McInnes' actions provoked what some have called a constitutional crisis when he relieved three premiers of their duties in the span of two years. In August 1898, he dismissed Premier John Turner because he believed Turner could not achieve a majority in the Legislature. McInnes was within his rights, but Professor Jackman believes the lieutenant-governor was "most ill-advised" to do so.[6] However, McInnes certainly believed he was justified when he asked Robert Beaven—then still a trustee of the Green Worlock estate—to form a government. When he could not do so, McInnes turned to Charles Semlin, who was soon defeated in the house, whereupon McInnes demanded his resignation. The Assembly passed a motion of censure against McInnes but he was undaunted in asking the unpopular Joseph Martin to form a government, which he could not do. In February 1900, when McInnes came to read the Speech from the Throne, most of the MLAs walked out. Hisses and catcalls came from the public galleries. It took three attempts for McInnes to finally completed his address.

Next, McInnes asked James Dunsmuir to form a government, a move that ultimately succeeded. McInnes' actions, however, were much criticized. When asked to resign by Prime Minister Laurier, McInnes refused, whereupon Laurier dismissed him in June 1900, thus ending "the most dramatic, sensational and significant scene in the whole history of British constitutional government," according to the *Colonist*.[7] In McInnes' defence, one historian claims it was "a political situation that would have taxed the ingenuity, patience and resourcefulness of the greatest of statesmen."[8]

The Duke and Duchess of Cornwall and York, *c.* 1901: A tour of the Empire, which included South Africa, Canada, Newfoundland, Australia, and New Zealand, aimed to reward the white dominions for their participation in the South African War, 1899–1902. Their presence at a glittering banquet in 1901 at Gyppeswyk (then serving as Government House) was a high point in the mansion's history.
VICTORIA *DAILY COLONIST*, OCTOBER 2, 1901, 1 AND 9

Perhaps in a show of indignation, McInnes and his lady took their time moving out of Gyppeswyk, but eventually settled back briefly on Michigan Street. They then travelled to New Zealand and Australia before making their way back to British Columbia. The couple settled in Vancouver, where McInnes set up practice both as a medical doctor and as a barrister, partnering in the latter with George Filmore Cane. The former vice-regal couple never returned to their original home in James Bay, probably to Martha's regret. But politics was in her husband's blood. In 1903, McInnes ran as an independent in a federal by-election in the Burrard riding. He came in third, but died soon afterwards in 1904.

Adding to the indignity of McInnes' exit from Gyppeswyk and the end of his vice-regal role was the decision not to commission an oil portrait of him in the lieutenant-governor's uniform, although the custom of doing so had already been established. A local writer has speculated that "Dr. McInnes was so enraged" by his dismissal that he refused to return to Victoria to sit for the painting.[9] It was not until 1957 that his portrait was created—from photographs.

The McInneses' Sons

Both the McInnes boys had active careers in the legal profession and in politics. They were also occasionally controversial, if not quite as much as their father. Living at Gyppeswyk from 1899 to 1900 with the lieutenant-governor and his wife, Martha, were their eldest son, Thomas Robert Edward MacInnes (who changed the spelling of the family name), his wife Laura (née Hostetter, of Toronto), and their ten-year-old son, Thomas Edward Loftus MacInnes. This boy—known as Loftus—was the second youngest person ever to live at Gyppeswyk.

Thomas Robert Edward MacInnes (1867–1950) was born in Dresden, Ontario, and was living with his parents at 110 Michigan Street when his father was appointed vice-regent. He served as his father's private secretary during his term as lieutenant-governor, a controversial appointment because, even in the later nineteenth century, it smacked of nepotism. He had completed a BA at the University of Toronto in 1889, then had studied law at Osgoode Hall, before being called to the bar in British Columbia in 1893. He went on to become a well-known lawyer and poet in British Columbia, exhibiting some of his father's truculence. (For instance, he was a member of the Canadian Union of Fascists and favoured exclusion of Asians from Canada.) His son Loftus (1891–1952) became a poet as well, and worked in the Department of Indian Affairs in Ottawa. He married the daughter of poet Archibald Lampman.

The McInneses' other son never lived at Gyppeswyk. William Wallace Burns McInnes (1871–1954) was named in honour of his family's Scottish heritage. As a law student, he had lived at home with his parents on Michigan Street but moved out when he married Dorothea Beynon Young in 1894. During his long career, "Billy" McInnes worked as a barrister, an MP, an MLA, and the provincial minister of education. From 1905 to 1906, shortly after Frederick Worlock left the territory, William served as commissioner for the Yukon. He also served as a Vancouver police magistrate (1944–54) and was notorious for passing severe sentences.

A Gentleman of France

Thomas McInnes' successor was an entirely different kind of man and much more successful. When Sir Henri-Gustave Joly de Lotbinière (1829–1908) retired as lieutenant-governor in 1906, an anonymous local poet ("H.E.K.") presented these lines "written for the *Colonist*":

Fare Thee Well!

Adieu, Sir Henri! You all hearts have won,
And here's a humble tribute to a setting sun
Which sinks in evening splendors, calm and bright,
And long will leave behind a gentle, lingering light:
The memory of a sunny smile, a kindly glance,
And courtly bearing of a Gentleman of France,
May favoring zephyrs waft you from the shore,
And all good guard you, till at length once more
You view the fair St. Lawrence, silver winding to the sea,
And tho' thousand miles, or more, will sever us from thee,
Still we hope there'll hide within your heart a memory of us yet,
Whilst we, who wish you now Godspeed, we never can forget.[10]

Although the poet exaggerates, Lotbinière was more popular and effective as vice-regent than his predecessor. As the poet implied, he was born in France on his family's estate, the son of pioneer photographer Gaspard Pierre Gustave Joly and his wife, Julie Christine Chartier de Lotbinière. His parents returned to their seigneury in Quebec in 1830, which Lotbinière inherited in 1860. Called to the bar in Quebec in 1855, he was eminently successful in politics, becoming a Liberal member of Parliament in 1867 and serving as premier of Quebec from 1878 to 1879. Later, he was a federal cabinet minister for four years, 1896–1900. He was an expert in constitutional matters, which would help him when he entered the confused situation in BC where he had to be conciliatory and objective in his dealings with the province's turbulent politicians.

Appointed to replace McInnes in June 1900, the new vice-regent and his wife had to live at the Driard Hotel while McInnes and his family slowly moved out of Gyppeswyk. Sir Henri had married Margaretta Josepha Gowen (1837–1904) in 1856, and together they had eleven children, though only six survived infancy. The children were all adults by the time their father became vice-regent so none lived at Gyppeswyk. For her part, Margaretta—described as "a lady of charm and courtly manner"[11]—made her mark as a patron of charities and literary societies. (Meetings of the local Shakespeare Club were held at Gyppeswyk during her residency). Unlike Mrs. McInnes, Lady Joly de Lotbinière was a great hostess.

A sense of the retinue required to maintain a well-appointed mansion—and a vice-regal one at that—a century ago can be gained from noting the servants who worked for the Lotbinières. In 1901, Hing Wee was the thirty-nine-year-old cook. Sing Lee, twenty years old, seems to have been his assistant. Mary Douglas from Scotland, aged twenty-eight, and Mary Thain from Ireland, aged twenty-four, were maid-servants. Twenty-two-year-old Hang Wing was a male servant. The preponderance of Chinese workers in Victoria's servant class is evident here as well. Some of these servants may have been permanent employees of Government House—wherever it was located—although the Lotbinières had more than previous vice-regal couples. We assume that several of them lived on Gyppeswyk's third floor.

Sir Henri Joly de Lotbinière: This portrait belies his personal charm, which restored the prestige of the lieutenant-governor's office after the "Ruritanian comedy" of Dr. McInnes' regime. He and his wife contributed dignified glamour to Gyppeswyk.

Lady Margaretta Josepha Joly de Lotbinière: While chatelaine of Gyppeswyk, Sir Henri's wife was not in good health but was a personable patron of the arts.
HP 054710 C – 07300, COURTESY OF ROYAL BC MUSEUM, BC ARCHIVES

At first, Lotbinière was not popular with British Columbians because many felt he had been imposed on the province after McInnes' shenanigans. As the poem quoted shows, however, he soon became one of the most revered vice-regents in BC's history. He continued the tradition of New Year's Day levees, which became perhaps even better attended during his tenure. One whole column of the Victoria *Daily Times* in January 1901 was required to list the names of the callers who came to Gyppeswyk to shake his hand on the first day of that year.[12] The name of Lotbinière Avenue, which flanks the west border of the Government House grounds, is further testament to his popularity.

Today, one can imagine elegant people descending the staircase in Gyppeswyk's foyer, even a prince in a glittering uniform and a princess in a sumptuous ball gown. It's not far wrong to envisage such a picture because the Duke and Duchess of Cornwall (later King George V and Queen Mary) attended a state banquet there in 1901. Their Victoria sojourn emphasized the city's role as both an outpost of the British imperium and a vital link in its defence and communications network. During their world tour of the British Empire, they arrived at Rithet's outer wharf on the *Empress of Asia* on October 1, 1901. A ceremonial arch, one of several, spanned Belleville Street in front of the Legislative Buildings, its banner reading "Outpost of the Empire Welcomes You." James Bay Bridge was embellished with smaller arches. Government and Yates Streets were festooned with bunting, flags, and evergreen wreaths. Bells were rung and cannons boomed. The Duke and Duchess did not stay overnight at Gyppeswyk but instead retired to the Mount Baker Hotel on Beach Drive.

Nevertheless, the mansion on Moss Street played a role in the festivities. On the evening of the banquet, soldiers lined the mansion's curving driveway as the royal carriage arrived and dropped the duke and duchess under the porte-cochère. In order to accommodate the sixty-eight guests, the dinner tables must have extended from the dining room into the drawing room. In attendance were the lieutenant-governor and his wife, Prime Minister Wilfrid Laurier, Prince Alexander of Teck, Sir Hibbert Tupper, Sir Henry Crease, Premier Edward G. Prior and his wife, Bishop and Mrs. Cridge, and Mayor Charles Hayward, among others.* On this occasion, "the table was prettily decorated" with clusters of silver candelabra lit electrically.[13] According to the formal custom of the time, "His Royal

---

* See Appendix I.

Highness took in [to the dining room] Lady Joly de Lotbinière, Sir Henri took in Her Royal Highness and Sir Wilfrid Laurier took in Mrs. Prior." If you have a strong imagination, you can stand in these rooms today and detect the perfume of floral decorations and hear the murmur of discreet conversation, the tinkle of crystal, and the gentle clank of cutlery. Smartly dressed servers would have brought in the dishes from the kitchen, where the regular staff must have been augmented. All were probably working hard! Along the driveway outside, "a guard of the Royal Engineers was mounted and remained on duty until after the party had left . . . after which they marched back to barracks."[14]

In June 1903, as the king's representative, Lotbinière dismissed Premier Edward Prior for conflicts of interest. He then called on Richard McBride to form a government, thus inaugurating one of the longest and perhaps most successful premierships in BC's history. As well, Lotbinière fostered progressive forest policies, and planted several fine trees on the grounds of the rebuilt Government House. The governor of California, knowing of the lieutenant-governor's expertise in silviculture, presented him with the two redwoods that still stand in front of the Pollard Gallery on Moss Street.[15]

Although Gyppeswyk had electricity, it seems there were no important structural changes made to the mansion during the lieutenant-governors' residency.

By the summer of 1903, the vice-regal mansion on Rockland Avenue had been reconstructed and was ready for occupancy—at which time Gyppeswyk passed back into the hands of members of Victoria's commercial nobility.

Yates Street, looking west from Government Street, *c.* 1900: When the Spencers moved into Gyppeswyk, downtown Victoria already had a bustling urban look, with hydro poles and electric streetcars, paved streets, and two- and three-storey buildings of brick and stone. David Spencer's department store contributed to the modernity of the city.

DAVID SPENCER AND HIS BUSINESS

From 1903 to 1951, members of the Spencer family lived at Gyppeswyk—first David and Emma and some of their children, then the widowed Emma and three of her daughters, and finally, after two of her sisters passed away, Sara Spencer alone. Their residency, longer than that of any of the other families who lived in the house, has left many referring to the structure as "the Spencer Mansion." Justifiably, for they put their mark on the house, and, even more so, on the city of Victoria itself.

An Outpost of Empire
When Welsh immigrant David Spencer arrived in Victoria in 1863, the city was in an economic slump. However, he had intelligence and ambition, and he gradually prospered, eventually outdoing both Alexander Green and Frederick Worlock.

When Spencer purchased Gyppeswyk in 1903, he had already been in Victoria for forty years. During that time, he had seen the city develop a character and an appearance that would define it for the rest of the twentieth century. Moreover, Victoria had just passed through an important period in its growth. In 1898, the imposing new Legislative Buildings had opened near Spencer's home on Birdcage Walk. The downtown, where he had his retail business, was no longer just a few blocks encompassing Government, Yates, and Wharf Streets. And with a population of 16,849, Victoria was still larger than Vancouver.

David Spencer in middle age: A bearded Victorian patriarch with "go-ahead" modern business practices, his department store was a Victoria institution for more than half a century.
HP077979 E-00526, COURTESY OF ROYAL BC MUSEUM, BC ARCHIVES

The city now enjoyed electric streetcar service—including the line up Fort Street past Moss Street to the newly opened Royal Jubilee Hospital. A few horseless carriages had appeared, and the city's main streets were being macadamized. In 1902, Government

Street was paved with concrete. That same year, a stone causeway replaced the James Bay Bridge over the Inner Harbour. Canadian Pacific steamships now connected the city to Seattle and Vancouver, and to the Far East. By 1908, construction of the Empress Hotel had begun on the reclaimed (and unlamented) James Bay flats. The hotel was to serve travellers and tourists arriving on those ships. Many more such structures were built of brick and stone, and both public and private life had a certain veneer of gentility. As the twentieth century dawned, semi-rural suburbs such as Rockland supported fine mansions like Gyppeswyk.

In fact, by 1903, Victoria was on the verge of an economic boom. The city already had the largest iron works on the Pacific coast outside San Francisco. Several factories were making boots, shoes, and cigars, and others were making wagons and carriages. A sawmill and a planning mill were also in operation, as were a box factory and a meat-packing house. As well, one could find bookbinderies, soap works, cracker bakeries, and a corset factory. In 1888, the Esquimalt and Nanaimo Railway had arrived. Electric lighting had been introduced, and free home delivery of mail had begun. In 1890, the City had begun to install the sewage system that would eventually serve Gyppeswyk.

Other civic improvements were also underway. In 1896, the Provincial Museum had opened. In 1891, the Public (Carnegie) Library was established. When Victoria College was founded in 1902, a campaign to have a local university was inaugurated. In 1911, construction began on a new four-storey high school on Fernwood Road; it became one of the most imposing structures in the community. In 1914, the Normal School for the training of teachers opened in an impressive, towered structure on a rise overlooking the city.

Even with all this change, the social and political atmosphere of the city remained resolutely British, as evidenced in how the city welcomed the Duke and Duchess of Cornwall in 1901. In addition, during the South African War (also known as the Boer War), which raged from 1899 to 1902, most Victoria residents heartily supported the British cause. The death of Queen Victoria in 1901 had occasioned much public grief. When the Canadian Pacific hotel opened on the Inner Harbour, its name alluded to the people of Victoria's attachment not only to the Empress-class ocean liners but also to the late queen/empress and to the British Empire itself.

As for Gyppeswyk, the mansion still stood in a sort of splendid isolation at the top of Moss Street. By 1905, a small, one-storey wing had been added to the northwest corner, the basis of the later laundry wing. Whether it was a Spencer addition or a facility built during the mansion's life as Government House is not known. For their part, the Spencers would make few changes to the house, besides the addition of the rear conservatory and the automobile garage on the north side. While David Spencer did not alter Gyppeswyk's fabric very much, he did transform Victoria's business centre.

David Spencer: Esteemed and Valued

In their old age, David Spencer and his wife, Emma, were described as two of Victoria's "most highly esteemed and valued citizens."[1] They had both, however, come from origins humbler than those of the Greens, the Worlocks, the McInneses, or the Lotbinières. David Evans Spencer was born in 1837, the son of a farmer, Christopher Spencer, and his wife, Ann Evans, who lived near St. Athan in the Vale of Glamorgan, near Cardiff in South Wales. Young David attended Cowbridge Grammar School, and then apprenticed in a draper's shop for several years, gaining experience that later stood him in good stead in Victoria. By the age of twenty-two, he had become a lay preacher in the local Wesleyan Methodist Church. Such community service and faith would characterize his entire life.

Meanwhile in British Columbia, the Fraser River Gold Rush began in 1858; then gold was discovered at Williams Creek in 1861, which touched off the Cariboo Gold Rush that ran until about 1865. In 1862, the London *Times* published letters from its correspondent in British

Victoria Library: An advertisement for Spencer's first endeavour, in the *British Colonist*, January 29, 1864 (2). A British observer, Matthew Macfie, wrote in 1865 about how this "reading room, well supplied with books and newspapers, is kept by an enterprising citizen, for admission to which there is a small charge."
VANCOUVER ISLAND AND BRITISH COLUMBIA, 79

Columbia. Inspired by reports of the wealth to be made in this western colony, thousands of men left Britain afflicted with gold fever. Spencer family lore maintains that William Wilson—later the founder of W. & J. Wilson, Clothiers, in Victoria—sent back to his brother Joseph in England enthusiastic reports about the wealth to be made in British Columbia. Spencer's brother John worked with Joseph, who shared the reports, and so Spencer and Joseph were inspired to leave together in search of gold, their destination being the Cariboo country.[2]

Sometime in 1862, twenty-five-year-old Spencer, presumably with a few pounds saved from his apprentice wages, set sail for New York with Joseph. From there (with or without Joseph), he sailed to Colon in Panama, crossing the isthmus by rail to Balboa, then continued

Victoria House: Spencer's original dry goods store, at the corner of Fort and Douglas Streets, opened in 1873. Already Spencer understood the value of large display windows with plenty of glass.
HP 089797 E-09075, COURTESY OF ROYAL BC MUSEUM, BC ARCHIVES

on to San Francisco by ship. He arrived in Victoria by the steamer *Pacific* in December 1863. The very next month, Spencer purchased his first business premises in Victoria.

Some confusion has arisen as to what Spencer was doing between leaving Britain and opening his shop in Victoria because some sources claim he left for Canada in 1862. This has led historian Peter Johnson to maintain that, after arriving in Victoria (possibly in the spring of 1863), Spencer went on to the Cariboo. Johnson suggests Spencer spent "less than a year" there but made enough money to return to Victoria and purchase a business.[3] However, the Spencer family maintained that he never went north, but that, after several weeks in Victoria, he simply realized he was not likely to strike it rich. Perhaps Spencer found that the colony was "a city full of disappointed men."[4] Or maybe he was daunted by the five hundred miles of difficult terrain that lay between Victoria and the Cariboo region.[5]

Like Alexander Green, David Spencer was very active in the affairs of Victoria. He belonged to the Wesleyan Methodist Church at the corner of Pandora Avenue and Broad Street, where he was a lay preacher, and where he taught (and later superintended) the Sunday school.[6] He and his wife both also preached to prisoners at the local jail. At various times, Spencer was church secretary and a member of its building committee. He loved music, and sang in (and later led) his church's choir. From 1865 to 1867, he conducted a singing class with a hundred students in the basement of the Methodist Church. And like Frederick and Ray Worlock, he was a member of the Arion Male Voice Choir.

In 1887, Spencer was a delegate to the organizational meeting of the BC Methodist Conference, held at the Pandora Street church. Several years later, as part of the festivities of the May 1906 Methodist Conference, which was also held in Victoria, he and his wife hosted a reception at "their beautiful residence" on Moss Street, which "promise[d] to be a very brilliant function . . ."[7] Otherwise, however, the Spencers do not seem to have played a large part in the meeting. By this time, the pair were already acknowledged to be pillars of their church, but were perhaps beyond the age of accepting extensive community responsibilities.

In any case, Spencer made a large cash donation toward the building of the new Metropolitan Methodist (later United) Church constructed on Pandora Avenue at Quadra Street in 1891. As well, he purchased land on Michigan Street and, in 1892, donated it to the Methodist authorities who built what later became the James Bay United Church, which Spencer and his wife attended when they lived on Belleville Street. Until the family moved to Gyppeswyk, several of his children sang in the church's choir. In fact, Christopher even continued as organist and choir leader until 1907 when he moved to Vancouver.

Like Alexander Green, David Spencer also seems to have had a strong social conscience. In 1871, he was even briefly a city alderman, but the cut and thrust of political life does not seem to have suited his character.[8] With Noah Shakespeare (1839–1921), who had been elected mayor in 1882, Spencer and his wife supported the Temperance Movement.[9] Spencer also served as treasurer of the Protestant Orphan Asylum Society, a role in which he would have known his James Bay neighbour Alexander Green. Furthermore, when Spencer died, his will specifically set aside money for the establishment of a tuberculosis ward at the Royal Jubilee Hospital.

David Spencer married Emma Lazenby in 1867 at the parsonage of their church on Pandora Avenue. As their family and their means expanded, they moved several times. Until about 1870, their home was a small cottage on Frederick Street.[10] After that they lived in a larger house at Cook and Yates for a while, but by 1874 they owned a home on the fashionable Menzies Street in James Bay.

Later that year, the Spencers built a two-storey, ten-room house at the south end of the James Bay Bridge on the southeast corner of Government and Belleville Streets, at 12 Belleville Street. Its bay windows, modest gingerbread trimming, curved interior staircase, and high ceilings were popular at the time. The quoins were painted darker than the white siding. Red, blue, and yellow glass surrounded the front door. Later the house became known as The Poplars because of the tall trees on the property. The Spencers lived there for twenty-five years. According to family lore, as David Spencer returned home for lunch each day, walking from his store across the James Bay Bridge, he could be seen by one or another of his children from their perch at the front window of The Poplars. Once warned that the patriarch had started across the north end of the bridge, Emma could have the table set and the meal ready when he walked through the front door. Even from a considerable distance, "Father" was easily recognizable in his frock coat and top hat.

The Poplars, which can be seen in some old photographs of Victoria and in an 1889 panorama of the harbour, was on the site now occupied by the BC Archives, just across Government Street from the Greens. The 1891 city directory lists all fifteen Spencers as living on

```
┌─────────────────────────────────────────────┐
│                                               │
│        SPENCER'S ARCADE.                      │
│        ────────────                           │
│        3 Cases New Goods this Morning.        │
│                                               │
│   Children's Silk Mother Hubbards, in all Shades, │
│            Children's Washing Dresses and Aprons, │
│                        Children's Jersey Dresses, │
│   Boys' Sailor Suits,                         │
│            Boys' Jersey Suits,                │
│                   Boys' Washing Suits and Blouses. │
│                                               │
│   The above are New Styles and Shapes, and are splendid value. │
│                                               │
│            ──────────────                     │
│            D. SPENCER,                        │
│                    Government Street.         │
│                                               │
└─────────────────────────────────────────────┘
```

Advertisement for Spencer's department store, 1889: The latest fashions, even for children, were supplied by Spencer's. Very possibly, Alexander and Theophila Green would have outfitted their children there.
COLONIST, MAY 28,1889, 3

Belleville Street in what must have been a full house. David Spencer built stables at 527 Michigan Street in 1897, and by 1918 had also erected a brick structure there for use as a garage for delivery vans.

In 1903, as the Lotbinières moved out of Gyppeswyk, the Spencers purchased the mansion from the Green-Worlock estate. They renamed it Llan Derwen, Welsh for "under the oaks," and moved in with ten of their brood. When the Spencers lived at Gyppeswyk, they offered a "quiet and informal hospitality."[11] They never served alcohol, avoided wearing clothes that might be considered ostentatious, and held prayers and sang hymns after dinner.

When David Spencer died in 1920, his widow and three daughters, Ada, Mary Louise, and Sara, kept living in the house. In 1934, when Emma Spencer passed away, her daughters remained at Gyppeswyk.

"If the character of people is respectable, humble origin is felt to be much less of a barrier to advancement in the colonies than in England,"[12] wrote British journalist Matthew MacFie about Victoria

After the Great Fire, 1910: Smoke was still rising from the smouldering ruins of the Five Sisters Block and Spencer's Arcade, but David Spencer had already placed a banner sign on the Driard Hotel announcing the continuation of his business!

HP 080720 E – 02696, COURTESY OF ROYAL BC MUSEUM, BC ARCHIVES

in 1865, inadvertently predicting the career of men like David Spencer. A typical nineteenth-century self-made man, Spencer ultimately attained a degree of wealth and social status that would have been nearly impossible for a man of his origins to achieve in Britain at the time.

Despite their great riches and their luxurious home at Gyppeswyk, David and Emma Spencer do not seem to have been members of the local social elite. Spencer had no position with the colonial government, the Royal Navy, or the Hudson's Bay Company. He was not one of those "gentlemen of the best education and ability" whom Sir James Douglas had required to help administer the colony.[13] In Victoria circa 1900, Spencer's position in trade rather than in the professions—or indeed in the inherited ownership of land—may have been held against him by some in Victoria's upper class. Furthermore, when David and Emma Spencer were living at Gyppeswyk, their Methodist beliefs would have distanced them from their nearest neighbours, the Church of England Creases at Pentrelew. On the other hand, the Spencers held a wealth and influence that the Creases, and many Anglicans, could not enjoy, which Victoria's influential class came to recognize over time. Still, at first, the Spencers were not entirely acceptable to the upper crust of the colonial aristocracy. Unlike Alexander Green, the son of a professional man, David Spencer was not the son of a gentleman but rather the offspring of Welsh farmers. He also lacked a university education. His neighbour Henry Crease was a lawyer and a judge, whose wife, Sarah, was the daughter of a gentleman. The Spencers would have had little to do with the Creases and their class. A telling example of David and Emma's exclusion from the highest social circles occurred during the Governor General's visit to Victoria in 1894. Invited to meet the Earl of Aberdeen and his wife, Lady Aberdeen, at a reception at Cary Castle on November 6th were Theophila Green, her eldest son, Ray Green, and her eldest daughter, Edna Theophila, even though the widow Green's husband had been dead for three years and his banking business was bankrupt. Also invited were Frederick and Martha Worlock, whose association with the failed bank was obviously not held against them. Absent from the guest list, however, were tradesman David Spencer and his wife. Although his establishment was already one of the largest and most successful commercial enterprises in British Columbia, Spencer's association with commerce or trade denied him and his wife an invitation to meet the queen's representative. (Also on the guest list was William Ridgway Wilson, a professional man and therefore acceptable.)

By the early twentieth century, the local aristocracy had become more accepting of folks in trade, but only if such work involved high finance or railway-building; retail trade—such as being the owner of a new-fangled department store as Spencer was—still had a certain stigma. Ironically, the Creases had constant difficulty maintaining their lifestyle, while the Spencers don't seem to ever have had to skimp in anything.

After his brief service as alderman in 1871, Spencer abandoned political pursuits. Not surprisingly, he was not active in the club life of Victoria's business elite. Nor does his name figure in the historical accounts of local high society, such as the Union Club or the Victoria Golf Club. When Vancouver publisher S.J. Clarke assembled biographies of BC politicians, businessmen, and professional men in two large volumes, *British Columbia: Pictorial and Biographical* (Vancouver, 1914), he included nothing on the already wealthy, successful, and famous Spencer. Nor did the *Daily Colonist* include the Spencers' mansion in its special 1903 supplement on "Beautiful Homes."[14] Furthermore, the Spencers do not seem to have had the fashionable Hannah Maynard take formal photographic portraits of themselves or their children. As for David Spencer's purchase of Gyppeswyk, it could well have been motivated as much by practical concerns as by status-seeking ones: its many rooms could house his large family.

David Spencer dedicated his life to philanthropy, the church, and his business. In the latter enterprise, he was remarkably successful, which the community eventually acknowledged. An indication of his perceived importance to Victoria was the guest list from his funeral, held at the Metropolitan Methodist Church on March 4, 1920. Present were Lieutenant-Governor Prior, several aldermen, and representatives from his stores in Victoria, Vancouver, and Nanaimo, who "filled the whole left section of the church."[15] By this time, his career in trade no longer seemed to matter much.

In his will, Spencer left bequests to his church, the Protestant orphanage, and the Royal Jubilee Hospital, but did not specify any bequests to his wife or children.[16] As a result, we must conclude that his offspring all had shares in the company—the sons, of course, were also employees of the firm. Perhaps Spencer assumed his daughters would marry and therefore be well looked after following his demise.

Instinctively Aggressive and Full of Enterprise

With these adjectives, the obituary writer for the *Colonist* defined the late David Spencer's business acumen,[17] a description that seems accurate. Perhaps as a youth Spencer had an intellectual, or at least a book-loving, bent because the small business he purchased from J. Corin in January 1864 was variously called a stationery store, a book-store, and "The Victoria Library." Unfortunately, this venture was not a success so Spencer sold his stock in 1872 to Hibben and Carswell, who became well-known stationers. By 1874, Spencer and William Denny were operating a small dry goods store, Victoria House, on Government Street near the corner of Fort Street. The chattering classes soon made this dry goods and carpet warehouse a popular gathering place. In 1878, Denny bought Spencer out, and continued independently, leasing a site he called "Commerce House," which was also on Government Street near the corner of Fort. Spencer was now on his way to becoming a "merchant prince," as he was described by contemporaries.

In 1882, David Spencer purchased an L-shaped property, where he built a two-storey structure, thus expanding his Government Street business to front onto Broad Street. The architect was Elmer Fisher.[18] As his business continued to grow, Spencer purchased another property adjacent to his store and erected a four-storey building designed by the architect Thomas Hooper.[19] This was the beginning of the famous Spencer's Arcade, which opened in 1885.

David Spencer was up-to-date on retailing matters. His expanding business was part of a new development in retailing in Europe and North America: department stores. Such enterprises often began, like Spencer's did, as dry goods establishments. At first, they sold ribbons, thread, lace, fabric, and patterns. But as a host city such as Victoria grew in population, the number and variety of customers encouraged store owners like Spencer to widen their stock. Meanwhile, better roads and the introduction of the electric streetcar were bringing more people to shop in city centres, which meant prosperity for merchants.

Eventually Spencer's store became one of Victoria's biggest importers, and largest employers, and probably had the largest sales volume of any store in the city. By 1896, the *Daily Colonist* would say that Spencer's store was "recognized as a leader in the retail dry goods trade."[20]

Obviously, David Spencer understood the economics of his business. He also understood the necessary technology with which to develop it. For example, he exploited recent advances in glass technology by installing big plate-glass front windows and a large skylight. Similarly, he saw to it that Spencer's Arcade was brightly illuminated by electricity. Expanding further in 1906, Spencer purchased the nearby Williams Block, then the *Daily Times* building in 1909. The whole enterprise had taken on a "metropolitan air," said the *Times*.[21] A sign of the business' growth was the fact that Spencer employed only six people in 1878, but by 1908 he employed two hundred and fifty.[22]

Spencer was now selling more than just dry goods: his business was developing into one of Canada's first department stores. Originally, he expanded by introducing carpets and Oriental rugs, then men's and boys' clothing, and then shoes. By 1891, he offered dressmaking and millinery, plus ladies' "bath gowns and tea gowns."[23] Eventually, his Victoria store had over thirty different departments.

When the Canadian Pacific Railway reached the coast in 1886, Spencer was one of the first local businessmen to board a train bound for eastern Canada. Travel for his business became a habit that took him to the United States, as well as to England, France, and Germany. (He maintained a buying office in London.) Atlantic passenger lists note that, even at seventy-two years of age, Spencer was travelling to Europe and back. (Eventually his sons took over these buying trips.) Meanwhile, the enterprise opened outlets in Nanaimo (1889) and Vancouver (after 1906), among other places. (The Vancouver store, enlarged in 1924–25, is now designated as a heritage building.) By 1891, Spencer's annual business already amounted to two hundred thousand dollars.[24]

Spencer's department store, Douglas and Yates: The new store, fronting on Douglas Street, with the old Driard Hotel in the background. The Bay Centre continues the commercial traditions established there by David Spencer.

HP 089816 E-09094, COURTESY OF ROYAL BC MUSEUM, BC ARCHIVES

Despite the modernity of his establishment's fixtures, and perhaps because of the piecemeal nature of its expansion, Spencer's premises—frame construction with a brick facade—were a fire trap. In October 1910, disaster struck as Spencer's department store was levelled in a fire. The loss was estimated at one million dollars. Spencer immediately leased the ground floor of the nearby Driard Hotel, the adjacent Imperial Hotel, and the Victoria Theatre, and refitted them for his business. Stock was brought in from Vancouver. Crews worked day and night for two weeks to refit the Driard. It was said that no Spencer employee lost even a day's work or salary because of the disaster. Eventually, David Spencer constructed a completely landmark new store fronting on Douglas Street. Later, he purchased the entire Driard property and adapted it for his business while the Arcade Block was rebuilt to serve as the store's annex.

Some of Spencer's business ventures may seem surprising but were probably influenced by his childhood experiences. He was raised by farming parents in the Welsh countryside and maintained an interest in agriculture all his life. Perhaps this is one reason why he operated a large farm in Haney (now part of Maple Ridge) in the Fraser Valley where dairy products were made and vegetables and fruit were grown for sale in his stores. He also operated a creamery in Kamloops as well as mines and a ranch in BC's interior.

In 1904, the business became incorporated as "David Spencer Limited," with the patriarch and his five sons each allotted one share. Despite this canny move, David Spencer Limited became known for business integrity, good customer service, and high-quality merchandise.

By the time of David Spencer's death in 1920, this joint-stock company advertised as "Home and Hotel Furnishers" or "Spencer's Department Store." The Victoria store stood on the site of the present-day Bay Centre on Douglas Street. There were also stores in Nanaimo, Vancouver, Chilliwack, Duncan, Mission, and Courtenay. In 1908, the Victoria, Vancouver, and Nanaimo stores together employed about five hundred and fifty people; by 1917, the Victoria store was the largest such store in western Canada and together with the Nanaimo and Vancouver stores employed nine hundred and fifty people.[25] Eventually the firm also owned the Victoria *Daily Times*.

Today, Spencer would be called a hands-on entrepreneur for taking an interest in every aspect of the business and to some degree personally supervising it. Even as an elderly man, he was said to be in the store "practically every day."[26] In late-nineteenth-century Victoria, the custom was to include your family members in your business—if at all possible—and often three or four members of the same clan could be found working together. Spencer's employment of his sons is a good example of this tradition. He kept the business in the family, with his offspring working first as clerks and buyers and then later as directors. For example, Christopher began as a clerk in his father's store in 1887; by 1890, he was a buyer, and by 1894, a manager. Victor, too, began as a clerk, in

1898; and throughout the 1890s, Thomas Arthur was also a clerk. The records do not suggest whether or not Spencer's sons enjoyed this work, but their later success in the business suggests that, at the very least, they accepted their fate and made the best of it. It is possible they inherited their father's business genes. Certainly they were regarded with affection by their employees, who referred to them as "Mr. Chris" and "Colonel Victor."

One of David Spencer's daughters, Agnes, also worked as a clerk in Spencer's Arcade from 1897 to 1900. In addition, Spencer hired his wife's twin sister, Eliza Lazenby (who lived with the Spencers for a while), to manage his millinery department. As late as 1899, even after she had become Mrs. John Teague, Eliza continued to run this department. Less deliberately, David Spencer presided over the marriage of his daughter Ann Elizabeth to Frank William Grant, one of his bookkeepers and later the manager of the Nanaimo branch of the store. (This wedding took place on Belleville Street where the Spencers were living at the time.)

David Spencer's social conscience was reflected in his business practices. He "never speculated to any extent," said the *Colonist*, but purchased property only as he needed it for his business.[27] (He did, however, own land between Gorge and Burnside Roads in Victoria.) As well, he did not offer credit, accepting only cash for purchases. The store published catalogues and had a mail order system. Plus, as a public service, his premises housed a library and a post office. For a while, the Young Men's Christian Association was provided with space on the second floor of his store. David Spencer Limited also sponsored a cricket team and, during the Great War, a Home Guard. On the occasion of the fiftieth anniversary of the opening of his first store, Spencer chartered the entire Victoria streetcar service so that everyone could ride free for a day. (The stunt was repeated in 1933.) Although a degree of bias may be present in the reports of Spencer's great integrity and fair dealing, little evidence exists to the contrary.

David Spencer Limited seems to have enjoyed good relations with its employees. Perhaps Spencer brought to the ownership of a large department store and the management of its employees some of the traditions of the master-apprentice relationship wherein both parties had obligations to each other. This mindset was already dying in the early twentieth century but Spencer would have experienced it as a draper's apprentice during his youth in Wales.

For decades, Spencer's Victoria department store was a central destination for the thousands of shoppers who traditionally went downtown for their purchases. Spencer's nine stores all survived the Great Depression and the Second World War. Unlike Alexander Green's business, David Spencer Limited long survived its founder's death, until hearty competition and rising taxes spelled the chain's doom. In 1948, Eaton's took over the Spencers' stores.[28]

One can only speculate and marvel at the different fates that lay in store for even the most enterprising of entrepreneurs and their families. After Alexander Green's death in 1891, his family gradually dispersed and his widow moved to smaller quarters. No one today calls Gyppeswyk "the Green Mansion"—although one could argue in favour of doing so—and Garesche Green & Co. is scarcely remembered. (Not surprisingly, the Green Block has no plaque or inscription mentioning Alexander Green.) On the other hand, David Spencer Ltd. was a striking success, not only during David Spencer's lifetime, but also after his death.

People used to say that behind every great man was a great woman. Many would agree that Emma Spencer filled that role perfectly. Our next chapter shows why.

EMMA SPENCER AND HER CHILDREN

Today we might describe Emma Spencer as a homemaker, but that word alone cannot encompass her role at Gyppeswyk for over thirty years. She was truly a chatelaine, supporting her thirteen children, encouraging her husband, leading several local charitable and religious enterprises, and running—albeit with the help of servants—a mansion that was not just a home but also a social centre. Indeed, in the half century that members of her family lived there, the house was described as "always a place of great activity."[1]

"Strong Character and a Sweet Disposition"[2]

In 1917, David Spencer and his wife, Emma, were declared to be "united in their interests and sympathies."[3] Mrs. David Spencer, however, should not be subsumed in her husband's identity, for she was herself a force to be reckoned with. Born in the parish of Bubwith, East Yorkshire, in 1843, Emma Lazenby arrived in Victoria in January 1863, having sailed from Gravesend in September 1862 with thirty-six other women from the Manchester area on the bride-ship *Robert Lowe*. This vessel was sponsored by the British Columbia Emigration Society, which aimed to provide respectable wives for the province's miners, thus establishing a more stable society. At only twenty-one years of age, Emma made the courageous decision to leave her family and her home and travel to a largely unknown

Emma Spencer in old age: The adventurous young woman who had arrived on a brideship became the mother of thirteen children and the chatelaine of Gyppeswyk, sharing her husband's social conscience and energy.

and possibly uncivilized country. On the other hand, this long and potentially dangerous voyage allowed her to escape what likely would have been a miserable life working in the factories of England during the Industrial Revolution. (The American Civil War had caused a decline in cotton shipments to British mills, throwing thousands out of work.) Emma's Methodist beliefs strengthened her social conscience—and her personal courage. She was at sea for one hundred and fourteen days.

Arriving in Esquimalt on January 10, 1863, Emma lived there for the first four years of her life in Canada. On her first Sunday in Victoria in 1863, she attended the Methodist church on Pandora Avenue, which is where she later met David Spencer. Becoming "one of the most able Sunday School Teachers,"[4] she was appointed the church's superintendant of social purity, in which capacity she helped to establish the Refuge Home for Chinese Girls, founded circa 1870 on Cormorant Street. (This quaint-sounding vocabulary belies her hard work and progressive values.) Emma was the first, and long-serving, president of the refuge home, which eventually included a maternity ward. In 1881, she joined the Women's Christian Temperance Union, and in 1889, was elected president of the local branch. She also supported the Women's Missionary Society. She and other Methodist women served tea in the basement of the Pandora Avenue church in the evenings to raise funds for the church's activities. The memoirist Edgar Fawcett jokingly called these events "tea fights." They were well attended, even at one dollar and fifty cents a person—perhaps because the "tables [were] spread with good things."[5] Emma's leadership role in the Methodist community was reflected in her being chosen to lay the foundation stone of the Centennial Methodist (later United) Church on Gorge Road in 1891.

Emma is reported to have said: "I never bothered much about the business or even talked to my husband about it. You see, I had thirteen children to look after and in our first years there was no help in the colony excepting the Indian women."[6] However, to raise thirteen

The Spencer family, *c.* 1885: Christopher, the first born, is in the centre, flanked by the twins, Mary Louise and Agnes; David Junior is on the right, with his hand on John William's shoulder; Thomas is on the left; Victor is leaning against his father's knee and is flanked by Anne and Josephine; and Charlotte sits on Emma's lap. Three more children were yet to be born.

offspring and, at the same time, carry on with dedicated service to her church and community would have required a mental and emotional discipline that probably contributed to her husband's success. Moreover, we can believe what one journalist said of the Spencers: "He made money; his wife saved it."[7]

In June 1917, Emma and David Spencer celebrated their fiftieth wedding anniversary with a luncheon at Gyppeswyk. In attendance were forty-five family members, including nearly all their sons and daughters as well as twenty-two of their grandchildren. (Absent were daughter Sara and grandson Evan David, who were both serving in the Great War in Europe.) Other guests included Dr. John Sebastian Helmcken, Edgar Fawcett, and former mayor Noah Shakespeare.

The Spencers' home on Cook Street: One of the Spencers' first modest homes, with what looks like an annex built to accommodate their expanding family. Another practical feature was the fenced-in vegetable garden in the front yard.

"The beautiful home," wrote the *Times*, "looked at its best in the warm sunshine . . . The house was prettily decorated for the occasion and musical selections had been arranged."[8] Congratulations were sent by the lieutenant-governor and Mrs. Francis Barnard, Premier Harlan Brewster, and Reverend Robert Wilkinson of the Methodist Conference of BC. David and Emma received many gifts including an engraved gold shield from the staff of the Victoria Spencer's store and five gold vases from the Vancouver staff.

On the occasion of Emma's eightieth birthday in 1922, more than seventy people, including the members of the board of the Metropolitan Methodist Church and their wives, arrived at the mansion to present her with a "beautiful illuminated address."[9] When David Spencer Limited celebrated its fiftieth anniversary on October 1, 1923, the by-then-widowed Emma formally opened the Victoria store with a golden key, receiving a "great ovation"[10] from the employees. In 1924, Emma graced the Reunion Ball of the Sons and Daughters of British Columbia held at the Empress Hotel with her "handsome presence."[11] The occasion was also her eighty-second

The Spencers' home on Belleville Street, The Poplars: A more substantial, ornate, and imposing structure than their previous homes, indicative of David Spencer's growing prosperity. Sir James Douglas' former home was behind the house and Spencer's business was a short walk across the James Bay Bridge to downtown. When this photo was taken, the Spencers had long since moved out and The Poplars had become a boarding house.

birthday. Similar accolades were made on her ninetieth birthday, when bouquets and telegrams arrived from the church, the Women's Christian Temperance Union, and the Women's Canadian Club.

Emma Spencer died at Gyppeswyk in 1934. At her funeral, the entire western section of the Metropolitan United Church was reserved for Spencer's employees, three hundred and twenty-five of whom attended. Sixty-five members of the Spencer clan were also present, as were members of the provincial government and local benevolent organizations. Another service was held at the mansion, conducted by Reverend Thomas H. McCrossan, one of Emma's sons-in-law.

Unlike the scions of some of Victoria's upper crust, the Spencers' sons were not sent to England for a public school education. Although wealthier than the Greens and many others in the commercial aristocracy, David and Emma Spencer had their children educated in Victoria. In fact, the 1901 census suggests that all ten of their unmarried children were still living at home on Belleville Street, which partly explains why David and Emma wanted larger quarters. Only Christopher, who was married and living next door on Birdcage Walk, and Josephine and Anne, who were also married, had left home by then. With its eight bedrooms, Gyppeswyk must have seemed big enough to house this large family. And so, in 1903, after several years of dignified adult occupation, Gyppeswyk once again resounded with the clatter and bustle of young people. David Junior, Agnes, and Mary Louise were in their thirties;[12] Thomas, William, and Charlotte were in their twenties; and Sara, Ada, and Florence were still teenagers. Even with eight bedrooms, Gyppeswyk must have been crowded when the Spencer family moved in. Some of the children would have had to share bedrooms. (But Sara, in her later years, had a room to herself on the south side of the mansion.)

Most of the Spencer children enjoyed music. Some were accomplished musicians and several were patrons of both music and the visual arts. Inevitably, given the customs of the time, the sons played a more extensive role in the business world.

"Capable and Energetic Boys"[13]

All of the Spencers' sons worked in the family business in some capacity, and most continued their parents' tradition of community service. Christopher Spencer (1868–1953), the eldest, never lived at Gyppeswyk, but he probably visited often enough with his own family and he may even have considered it a second home. He was born in the Spencers' first residence, which was above his father's store on Government Street. He was the first to leave home and was living on Princess Street with his new wife, Sara Ellen Evans, whom he married in 1891. By 1893, Christopher and Sara had moved to Superior Street and back into his parents' James Bay orbit. In 1897, they were living on Birdcage Walk, again not far from the Spencers.

The Spencers' fiftieth wedding anniversary, 1917: Lieutenant-Colonel Victor Spencer, sitting to his mother's right, is in military uniform. To Emma's left is the venerable David Spencer, now in poor health. Carpets were spread on the driveway. At the rear are the library windows. To the left is part of the porte-cochère. Among the grandchildren in the front row are a future Nobel Prize winner and a famous artist. Visits from this generation to Gyppeswyk must have made the mansion a lively place.

HP 031121 B-02244, COURTESY OF ROYAL BC MUSEUM, BC ARCHIVES

Even as a teenager, Christopher had been entrusted several times by his father with the management of the store when the latter was out of town. After leaving Victoria High School, "Mr. Chris" entered the family business at the age of fourteen—about the same age his father was apprenticed to a draper back in Wales. By 1889, Christopher, described as "dignified and courtly,"[14] was a buyer in his father's business. In 1907, he moved to Vancouver to manage the Spencer's store there. By 1920, his father having passed away, he was company president and lived in Kerrisdale, where he entertained guests with his pipe organ. Proud of his Welsh heritage, as his father had been, he named his Vancouver home Ty-Celyn (or "house in the holly"). Christopher was involved in several other businesses and served for a while on the University of British Columbia's board of governors. In 1948, he was named a Commander of the Most Excellent Order of the British Empire.

One of Christopher's sons, Evan David Spencer (1897–1918), became an accountant, and was a lieutenant with the Canadian Railway Corps then later with the Royal Air Force during the First World War. He was killed in France in June 1918.

From 1887 to 1892, David Scott Spencer ("David Junior") (1869–1932), who lived for a time at Gyppeswyk, worked as a clerk in his father's store. He had attended the Boys' Central School on Fort Street, not far from Gyppeswyk, then had trained with a London business firm, after which he took a position in Spencer's office there. Although later he assumed the title of director in David Spencer Limited, he was not usually active in the family business. Described as "a rollicking, genial soul," his generosity was legendary. It was said that on cold and rainy evenings he would buy the entire stock of a newsboy's papers to help the lad get home sooner.[15]

Like his father, and Alexander Green, David Junior succumbed to gold fever. And like Frederick Worlock, the Klondike Gold Rush drew David Junior to the Yukon in 1897. With nineteen other "sturdy and indomitable" local men, he proved "his sterling grit on the mountain march." Unfortunately, he fell ill with typhoid and pneumonia, and was hospitalized in Dawson City. Nevertheless, he staked claims on Moosehorn and All Gold Creeks, and, in May 1898, announced in a letter to his father that he was coming home "with a quantity of gold."[16] By 1899, David Junior was living in his parents' home on Belleville Street, but he enjoyed travelling, which perhaps explains the occasional absence of his name from the Victoria city directories of this period. In 1909, he was living with his parents and some of his siblings on Moss Street. Following his marriage in 1910, his residence changed to the October Mansion, an elegant new apartment building at Cook and Fort Streets. From 1913 to 1915, he lived at the Empress Hotel, presumably with his wife.

Methodist Conference at Gyppeswyk, 1906: The southeast conservatory was still in place. Gyppeswyk's new owners had not yet added the southwest conservatory or the laundry wing on the west side. A wire mesh fence had been constructed between the mansion and the grounds, perhaps for livestock control. A croquet game was interrupted for the photographer. The gentleman on the right stands by a wicket, still holding a croquet ball in his left hand.

If it is true that David Senior's private life was "marked by the highest domestic virtues,"[17] David Junior may have caused some scandal in 1910 when, at the age of forty-one, he married Kate Gordon (a twenty-three-year-old divorcee) in Vancouver—especially since David had been the co-respondent in Kate's divorce.

In 1918, David Junior purchased the home of architect Henry Sandham Griffith (1865–1943) at 2906 Cook Street, which was known as The Rocks or, as locals soon began to call it, "Spencer's Castle." His purchase of Griffith's impressive hilltop mansion was a display of status, and slightly out of keeping with his father's more modest inclinations. (When his widow sold it in 1964, the "castle" and its gardens were intended to become a public attraction.) The 1911 *Who's Who in Western Canada* tells us that David Junior's "recreations" were fishing and riding. He died at age sixty-two after a prolonged illness. Kate outlived her husband by forty-four years.

Thomas Arthur Spencer (1874–1940), who was sometimes called "Deans," also worked for his father as a clerk (at least in 1899) and lived at Gyppeswyk. By 1908, he was a manager at his father's store in Vancouver and a director of the business. That same year, he married Catharine Isabel Potts and they lived at the Majestic Apartments on Broughton Street. By 1913, the couple was living on Hollyburn in West Vancouver, in a house possibly designed by Samuel Maclure. Thomas Arthur was an enthusiastic horticulturist.

Educated at Victoria High School, John William(s) Spencer (1876–1946) was working in Spencer's Arcade by 1899. In 1905, he was in charge of the carpet department. He was described as "a quiet little man who saw everything and knew everybody."[18] He later became a director and secretary-treasurer of the business. During John William's tenure as director of the Victoria base of the business, David Spencer Limited took over Weiler's, at Government and Broughton Streets, and began using the premises as the china department. Around 1940, the former Mitchell and Duncan, a jewellery store at Government and View Streets, became a showcase for Spencer's fine silverware. At around the same time, fluorescent lighting was installed throughout the store.

John William was also a director of the Victoria *Daily Times* (which his family owned) and worked with the BC Power Corporation, Excelsior Life, and the Royal Trust. At various times, he was president of the Victoria Chamber of Commerce and the local Kiwanis Club, treasurer of the Victoria YMCA, and on the council of the Victoria Board of Trade. He supervised Vancouver Island's Victory Loans during the First World War. Like several other Gyppeswyk residents, he was a tenor member of the Arion Male Voice Choir, 1906–1910.

John William lived at Gyppeswyk with his parents until 1909 when he married Lillian Lemon Watts and moved to Joan Crescent. As proud of his heritage as his brothers were, he gave his home a Welsh name: Hael-y-Bryn, meaning "brow of the Hill." He and his wife often entertained at their country home in Saanich, most notably during the Second World War when they hosted parties for servicemen. His daughter Myfanwy Pavelic (1916–2007) became a famous Canadian artist, who created an excellent portrait of Colin Graham, a later resident of Gyppeswyk and the first curator/director of the Victoria Arts Centre. An exhibition of Myfawny's work at Gyppeswyk in 1964 drew large crowds. Wilspencer Place, adjacent to the art gallery, is named for her father.

Joseph Victor Norman Spencer (1876–1960) does not seem to have lived in his parents' Moss Street home for long, if at all. In 1907, he was manager of the Spencer's store in Vancouver. By 1910, he was living in the same apartment building as his brother Thomas and Thomas' wife. Victor later became vice-president and director of Spencer's in Vancouver. He married Gertrude Isabel Winch in 1913. The couple lived at Aberthau, a large neo-Tudor home in Vancouver's Point Grey neighbourhood. Victor had a great interest in cattle-raising, maintaining the family ranch in the Sumas area, and experimenting with growing tobacco and sugar beets. The gold that had originally inspired his father may have played a role in the development of his gold mines. He was "the handsome one for whom the belles of the late 'nineties sighed."[19]

Of all the Spencers' sons, only Victor diverged (albeit briefly) from working in business. At the age of eighteen, he enlisted as a trooper in Lord Strathcona's Horse and was sent to fight in the South African War, serving as a colonel. In 1914, at thirty-two years of age, he once again enlisted, this time as a captain in the Canadian Expeditionary Force at Valcartier, Quebec. He fought in several major First World War campaigns, rising to be named lieutenant-colonel and assistant quartermaster-general.

The Spencer Daughters

Six of David and Emma Spencer's daughters lived with them at Gyppeswyk. Three, in fact, lived out their lives there. The twins, Mary Louise (1873–1951) and Agnes Evans (1873–1943), were spinsters who lived most of their adult lives in the mansion with their unmarried sister Sara. Unlike her sisters, Agnes achieved some independence by working as a clerk for many years. Several of the Spencer daughters were talented musicians. For example, we know of a 1915 New Year's concert given by "the Misses Spencer" for local soldiers based at Willows Park. This performance was given in the Victoria Theatre, which their father had purchased and incorporated into his new department store.

Ann(ie) Elizabeth (1871–1954?) never lived on Moss Street. In 1894, she married Frank William Grant, a bookkeeper in Spencer's Arcade. They lived in Victoria, so they must have been frequent visitors to her parents' home. The far-flung addresses of the other married daughters are evidence of David Spencer's extensive business connections. Josephine Hortense (1878–?) married Thomas H. McCrossan of Minneapolis (and later of Albany, New York, and Seattle, Washington) on June 1, 1898, just before her father purchased Gyppeswyk. Her other sisters who married did so from the Rockland mansion, but then left the city to live elsewhere with their husbands.

Like most of the Spencers' daughters, Charlotte Emma (1880–1975) was taught at home by a private tutor. But she inherited her father's love of singing, as well as a certain talent for it (she had a mellifluous mezzo-soprano), and spent seven years studying voice in Germany. In 1917, she married Gerald Grattan McGeer, a lawyer, member of the BC legislative assembly for Richmond, and later mayor of Vancouver.

Florence Georgina (1889–?) married Arthur Graham Gray of Toronto in 1916. Ada Eliza (1887–?) became Mrs. Charles Vernon Vickrey of Scarsdale, New York, in 1912. Her husband was a Congregational minister who was very involved in missionary work and in the relief efforts during the Armenian crisis of 1912–1914. The gene for business sense appears to have re-emerged in their son, William Spencer Vickrey (1914–1996), a professor who shared the Nobel Prize in Economics in 1996. Like his parents and grandparents, he was a devout Christian, in his case, a practising Quaker and a conscientious objector during the Second World War.

Of this large cohort of siblings, many Victoria people remember most vividly Sara Ellen (1885–1983), who lived to be ninety-seven years of age. She was, like her father and several of her siblings, a dynamic personality—or, as a local journalist described her, "an outspoken woman of discerning taste and deep convictions."[20] Although she shared Gyppeswyk with her sisters Ada and Mary Louise, the mansion appears under only her name in most of the later city directories. She was a student in the first class of Victoria College, which at that time was located in Craigdarroch Castle, a short walk from her home. She was an equestrian, probably using the stables the Greens had bequeathed to posterity.

During the First World War, Sara was made an honorary lieutenant for her "magnificent" work with the Canadian Field Comforts Division at Shorncliffe, England—one of only seven Canadian women to attain this rank.[21] She also served as president of the Victoria Symphony Society and was involved with the Red Cross and the Community Chest (United Way). In 1960, her donation funded the construction of the Memorial Chapel at the Metropolitan United Church. After the death of her brother Will in 1946, Sara served with Christopher, Victor, and two others as a director of the Victoria Spencer's store until 1948. She also played a role in managing the Victoria *Daily Times*.

Sara Spencer was also active on the Victoria Arts Centre's board and served as president in 1952. It may have been Sara who inspired the showing of works by A.Y. Jackson and F.H. Varley at the Spencer's store in 1946—an exhibit that was seen by a young Colin Graham. Later on, she was appointed lifetime "honorary vice-president" of the art gallery's board of directors. As chatelaine of the mansion after 1934, Sara opened her home for social events organized by her many charitable causes. The last such event was a reception in September 1951 held in honour of the Victory Symphony's inaugural concert of the season, which was attended by Lieutenant-Governor Clarence and Mrs. Wallace.

Sara Spencer: She inherited her parents' dynamism, love of the arts, and sense of social responsibility. Her gift of the family home to Victoria for use as an arts centre ensured Gyppeswyk's survival.

The Spencer obelisk at Victoria's Ross Bay Cemetery: At their burial plot in Ross Bay Cemetery, the Spencers' sober grey granite obelisk contrasts with the Greens' more opulent red marble monument.
ROBERT RATCLIFFE TAYLOR

That same year, when Sara decided to live at 3610 Cadboro Bay Road, it must have seemed logical for her to donate the family mansion to the City for use as a gallery since her will also included a generous bequest to the art gallery. As a result, building on her membership in the Order of the British Empire, Sara was awarded the province's centennial senior citizen medal in 1958, at the opening of the art gallery's first addition. She was grateful, but said, typically, "It's too much honour, and much, much too much publicity."[22] Today, a portrait of Sara painted by her niece Myfanwy Pavelic hangs in Gyppeswyk's foyer, near the entrance to the former drawing room, which is now the Sara Spencer Gallery.

The Spencers were not the only ones living in the often crowded and busy Moss Street mansion from 1903 to 1951. Like previous residents of Gyppeswyk, they had several female servants as well as their choice of cook and gardener from Victoria's large pool of male Chinese labour, although these men may not always have lived in the house. In the later 1940s, the meals eaten by Sara and her twin sisters were prepared by Ho, who lived on the second floor of Gyppeswyk in a suite of rooms on the northwest side of the mansion. His cookery is described by Sylvia Graham as very good and enlivened by a herb garden he maintained on the property.[23] Allowing a servant—Chinese or white—to live on the same floor as their employers was a liberal act on the part of the Spencer siblings, but consonant with their humane and charitable beliefs. To a degree, of course, their attitudes were abreast of the times. In the fifty years since Gyppeswyk had been built, the servant class had almost disappeared. Good help was hard to find because two world wars, political revolution, and the Great Depression had liberated many in service. Meanwhile, a degree of social equality had become more of a reality (in Canada, at least) so it was no longer acceptable for upper-class folk to regard servants as subhuman.

In the last years of the three Spencer daughters' residence in the mansion, another Chinese servant, Sam, lived in a basement room, worked in the garden, and shovelled coal for the fireplaces. Ho and

Sam may even have served the family when Sara was young, living with her mother and sisters, but the records are not clear.

The Spencers seem to have had little interest in the finer points of interior design—the mansion's decor during their long residence has been described as "drab" and "depressing."[24] Perhaps the look of the rooms had changed much since the Greens lived in the house. The Spencers were not, however, a dour family: they played billiards on the table in the attic, and tennis and croquet outdoors. But practicality ruled when it came to home improvements. While Emma and David Spencer added the laundry wing and conservatory to the west side of Gyppeswyk, they did not make many other structural changes to the building. Between 1906 and 1917, though, they had the entire exterior painted white. At a certain point in the twentieth century, the modernizing of structures by whitewashing them seemed both sensible and fashionable. Moreover, to find painters willing to take the time to repaint the house's three different earthtones and repair the peeling walls would have been expensive. As practical as her parents, when Sara lived alone in the mansion, she used the original dining room as a smaller morning room, while the morning room served as her dining room because it was closer to the kitchen.

Greater in number than the Greens and more profoundly influential in Victoria's development, the Spencers could be considered one of the great dynasties of twentieth-century British Columbia. One historian's hyperbole is understandable when he describes the Spencers as "not merely a tribe, but a nation."[25] Their business, charitable, and cultural impacts were considerable. The achievements of Sara Spencer alone culminated in the establishment of Victoria's art museum.

A SHOWPLACE MANSION

After Sara Spencer vacated Gyppeswyk in the fall of 1951, the mansion became the home of a dynamic young couple, Colin and Sylvia Graham, who were to have a profound impact on the house and its role in Victoria's history. In leading the transformation of Gyppeswyk into a successful museum and centre for the arts, the Grahams also helped Victoria grow into a more sophisticated community, a development that might not have been predicted in 1951. Indeed, at the time, many people still regarded the city as a cultural backwater.

"The Most Hopeless Place Artistically in the Dominion"[1]

This is how Emily Carr described Victoria toward the middle of the twentieth century. In truth, local taste in the visual arts—painting and sculpture—was still rooted in the nineteenth century. However, musical performance had been assiduously cultivated since the founding of Fort Victoria, and Carr herself played guitar and mandolin, and had a good singing voice. By her time, choral and church music attracted many participants and Gilbert and Sullivan operettas were popular. We have already seen how the Greens, the Worlocks, and the Spencers were talented and enthusiastic musicians. Perhaps Carr's view was blinkered by her overriding interest in painting. In any event, shortly after she died in 1945, Victoria was transformed by the famous post-war boom that would ultimately help the visual arts flourish.

Douglas Street near Yates Street, *c.* 1949: Gas-fuelled buses had replaced electric streetcars; the modernization of older buildings was taking place; and the first high-rises were going up. The Hudson's Bay Company department store (built 1914–1921) can be seen at the far left. It was to this city, which some called a cultural backwater, that young Colin Graham arrived in 1951 to direct the Victoria Arts Centre at Gyppeswyk.

I-26498 04356, COURTESY OF ROYAL BC MUSEUM, BC ARCHIVES

There were negatives that came with the boom, of course. The early 1950s marked the beginning of an era in which the distinctiveness of Victoria would be challenged by suburban shopping malls, large paved parking lots, and widened asphalt streets. It was also a period during which heritage architecture, such as Gyppeswyk, could be damaged or even lost. In population, commerce, and industry, the city had been overtaken by Vancouver, which was now the province's metropolis. Many developments that seem questionable today were seen then as progress. In 1944, for example, the city began dismantling the streetcar system as gasoline-powered buses were introduced. (The last streetcar ran on July 5, 1948.) On the other hand, interesting new buildings were erected. In 1949, the Memorial Arena opened, dedicated to the fallen of the Second World War. In 1951, BC Electric opened its modern headquarters, an early high-rise tower on Blanshard Street. That same year, the Tillicum drive-in cinema began operation. Victorians were impressed by the fact that their homes were being transformed with electric stoves and oil furnaces. Television sets dominated living rooms. The city's population in 1951 was 104,303, but it was about to grow again.

Certain things, however, did not change. Some industry remained on the harbour, with lumber mills and other establishments continuing to belch out smoke and contaminants. Log booms clogged the upper harbour and railway tracks laced their way along the shore. Fish plants, shipyards, a grain elevator, and a paint factory were some of the bustling industries on the waterfront. The Victoria Machinery Depot had famously built ten-thousand-ton "Victory Ships" during the Second World War and Esquimalt continued to function as Canada's western naval establishment.

Although the ethnic background of its inhabitants would change drastically in the next decades, Victoria still vigorously touted its "Britishness." The Empress Hotel remained an iconic symbol of the CPR and the British imperial connection. Posters urged tourists to "Follow the Birds to Victoria," which proclaimed itself to be "a little bit of Olde England." Significantly, Princess Elizabeth and Prince Philip visited Victoria in 1951 to scenes of great enthusiasm.

Clearly, Victoria circa 1950 was a city of contrasting qualities. Above all, it was quieter and more conservative, but also more relaxed, than neighbouring Vancouver and Seattle. And therein lay its most significant aspect: as Colin Graham said in October 1951, the city was "unique in having preserved the essential dignities of human life."[2]

Colin Graham, *c.* 1952: The first curator/director (1951–73) of the Victoria Arts Centre, later called the Art Gallery of Greater Victoria, and, with his wife Sylvia, briefly a resident at Gyppeswyk. He was instrumental in making the local art gallery one of North America's finest—and in integrating Gyppeswyk with the modern additions.

Sara's Gift

For many years, Victoria's art lovers and artists alike had been seeking a proper site for the display of artworks—somewhere to establish a local civic art gallery. In 1946, the Little Centre was opened on Yates Street and in 1949, the arts centre operated at 823 Broughton, near the Royal Theatre. In 1944, artist Josephine Crease had offered her family home, Pentrelew, which was a stone's throw from Gyppeswyk, for use as an art gallery. However, the city fathers declined the gift and Pentrelew was eventually demolished in 1986.[3] Another suggestion was that the arts centre move into part of the expanding public library, but the library board rejected the idea.

Then, on July 21, 1951, the local press announced that Sara Spencer had donated her family home to the City of Victoria for use as an arts centre. By this time, Sara was sixty-three years old and her twin siblings, Mary Louise and Agnes, had passed away. For nearly fifty years of her life, she had lived at Gyppeswyk. Of course, she had memories of The Poplars on Belleville Street, but she must have been intimately attached to what many were then calling simply the Spencer Mansion. Long active in the cultural and philanthropic life of the city and sensing Victoria's desperate need for a proper arts centre, she freely donated her home to her fellow citizens and planned to move out. Thanks to Sara Spencer's gift, Gyppeswyk escaped the fate of the Crease family home.

The existing arts centre board of directors recorded their "deep appreciation" for Sara's "very exciting and generous offer."[4] For the exhibition of art works, Gyppeswyk seemed more suitable than the cramped inelegant downtown quarters. Despite its age, the house was still in good repair and had retained its architectural dignity and integrity. In 1917, the Victoria *Daily Times* had rightly called Gyppeswyk and its grounds "one of the beautiful old spots of the city"[5]; in 1951, the house was viewed, in John Adams' words, as "a showplace mansion."[6] Its sweeping driveway and porte-cochère gave Gyppeswyk's front facade a ceremonial but welcoming look. Its foyer, drawing, dining, and morning rooms were large enough for receptions or meetings of up to two hundred people. The main-floor library could function as a comfortable office, while the bedrooms upstairs could provide additional office or teaching space. There was not extensive wall space but the high ceilings and abundance of light were appealing.

Because of the mansion's historical associations, provincial archivist and librarian Willard Ireland recommended the City accept the gift of Gyppeswyk. That way, the house could be preserved and not become "a rooming house," he said. A proper modern gallery could later be built on the grounds.[7]

When she offered to donate her house to the City, Sara Spencer suggested—and the arts centre board concurred—that Gyppeswyk be held in trust for the arts centre, which would operate it as an art gallery. She also suggested the City could pay the property taxes (at that time, eight hundred and seventy dollars) and maintain the exterior of the structure and the grounds. The two lots of Garry oak woodland to the south of the mansion, which were included in the gift, might be maintained by the Parks Department at a cost of fifteen hundred dollars. The City was also encouraged to provide an annual grant of at least three thousand dollars to the arts centre to run the gallery and an additional two hundred and fifty dollars annually to cover the upkeep of the house.

"A Long and Complicated Story"[8]

Sara Spencer's proposed donation was met with disapproval among some the City aldermen who, wrote a local journalist, "were not overly anxious to take possession."[9] Nevertheless, in September 1951, after a long and heated meeting, the colourful incoming mayor, Claude Harrison, and the rest of Victoria City Council resolved to assume trusteeship for the mansion, but it was decided the City would provide only two hundred and fifty dollars for the regular upkeep of the exterior and grounds. The mayor and the council had balked at providing any larger annual grants. The arts centre would have to cover the property taxes. To be fair, this parsimony reflected local attitudes toward the visual arts and toward the notion of a publicly funded civic art gallery. In fact, one letter to a local newspaper declared that the Spencers themselves should have provided funding to maintain Gyppeswyk; another thought that using the mansion as a gallery would be "disastrous."[10]

Official opening of the Victoria Arts Centre, 1952: Half a century after the future king and queen of Canada dined at Gyppeswyk, Governor General Vincent Massey formally inaugurated the mansion's new life as a civic art museum. The Royal Canadian Navy played a salute (the first six bars of "God Save the Queen") as His Excellency arrived in the late morning of October 15, 1952.

Needless to say, the arts centre board was dismayed by the City's attitude. Colin Graham even wrote to a local artist that they were "terribly ashamed and embarrassed at the attitude the City Council was taking"—he believed their stance was an "extraordinary discourtesy toward a most generous and public-spirited gesture."[11] In the meantime, the provincial government began providing annual grants to the arts centre. Interestingly, in July 1952, it was discovered that the provincial Municipal Act contained no provision for the City of Victoria to make grants of any size to an arts centre, nor did the City have any legislative authority to accept in trust any building for use as a gallery. However, in January 1953, the provincial legislature

In Gyppeswyk's foyer, October 15, 1952: After his tour of the Spencer Mansion, Governor General Massey made his address to members of the Victoria Arts Centre, formally opening the new gallery. As photographed from the staircase.

rectified the situation by passing a bill allowing the City to hold the house in trust, which in turn allowed it to make grants to the arts centre. And so, thanks to small government grants, augmented by membership sales and admission fees, the arts centre was able to operate Gyppeswyk legally as an art gallery.

But a few snags still remained with regards to the mansion's ownership. "An embarrassing situation"[12] soon arose because, technically, the Spencer family still owned Gyppeswyk and were thus responsible for the property taxes. By November 1954, back taxes to the sum of two thousand dollars were owed to the City, which would have made the mansion eligible for seizure and sale to cover the debt had the trustees of the Spencer Foundation not delayed the transfer of ownership to the cash-strapped arts centre until November 1956.

The Victoria Arts Centre opened in Gyppeswyk informally on November 20, 1951 with an exhibit of loaned works that included Peter Lely's portrait of Charles II, Francis Gerard's portrait of a Roman general, and several paintings donated by Mark Kearley, a long-time supporter of the gallery project. Contemporary Québecois paintings, including works by Riopelle, Mousseau, and Borduas were also shown, although the *Times* art critic had her doubts about how the latter paintings would be accepted in conservative Victoria.[13] The new curator (and, later, director), Colin Graham conducted a tour.

On October 15, 1952, fifty years after BC's lieutenant-governors lived at Gyppeswyk, another vice-regal representative, Governor General Vincent Massey, presided over the official opening of the new Victoria Arts Centre. The exterior walls of the house were decorated with bunting, the galleries were bedecked with flowers, and in the late morning, the Royal Canadian Navy band played ceremonial music. J. Ronald Grant, president of the arts centre board, introduced Massey to local MLAs, Mayor Harrison,[14] three local reeves, Colin Graham, and Sara Spencer. Using a gold key presented by Spencer, the Governor General opened the main door. After the band played "O, Canada," Massey toured the galleries. Following the tour, Grant recounted the history of the arts centre and the Governor General addressed members of the centre in the foyer before signing the new visitor's book. Gyppeswyk had formally become Victoria's art gallery.

The Spencer family remained dedicated supporters of the arts centre. In the early 1950s, David and Emma Spencer's granddaughter Myfanwy Pavelic had a one-person show of her oil portraits at the arts centre. In 1970, Sara Spencer's name was listed as a "general donor," while the widows Lillian Spencer (Mrs. Will) and Kate Spencer (Mrs. David Junior) were credited for generous donations toward the construction of a new wing.

A Natural Ease and Charm

As curator of the Victoria Arts Centre, Colin Graham set about laying the foundation for a fine collection of art with a special focus on Asian pieces. Known for his "natural ease and charm,"[15] it is doubtful that the arts centre would have survived had it not been for the work of this enthusiastic and talented man. Although Graham lived in Gyppeswyk for only a year or two, he put his stamp on the house during the more than two decades that he led the institution. Most justifiably, one of the new Centennial Galleries has been renamed for him and his wife, Sylvia. As well, in 2011, sculptor Armando Barbon created a bronze bust of Graham, which now stands in the main lobby.

Born and raised in Vancouver, Colin Graham (1915–2010) attended Shawnigan Lake School on Vancouver Island. As was the case with the first owner of Gyppeswyk, his father was a medical doctor (an ear-eye-nose specialist)[16] and, like Alexander Green, Graham first enrolled in pre-medical studies. But after two years at the University of British Columbia he, too, changed direction, deciding to study medieval history at Gonville and Caius College, part of Cambridge University, and graduating with a BA in 1939. After studying for a PHD at Stanford University in 1940–41, Graham served with the special wartime division of the Department of External Affairs during the war. (Recurrent hepatitis, with its attendant fatigue, barred him from active military service. It would also later impel him into early retirement.) In 1949, Graham completed an MA in art at the University of California at Berkeley and became educational director of the California Legion of Honor, the civic art museum in San Francisco. He also gave courses for art educators at the California School of Fine Arts, where Emily Carr once studied.

When he learned that the Victoria Arts Centre was advertising for a curator, Graham applied for the position, which was to begin in October 1951. He planned to stay for two years, then resume teaching. As it turned out, his mother learned he had the job before he did. The board of directors announced his appointment

One proposal for the addition, *c.* 1956: In a style totally contrasting that of the mansion, but fireproof and allowing the preservation of the porte-cochère and the driveway.
ART GALLERY OF GREATER VICTORIA ARCHIVES

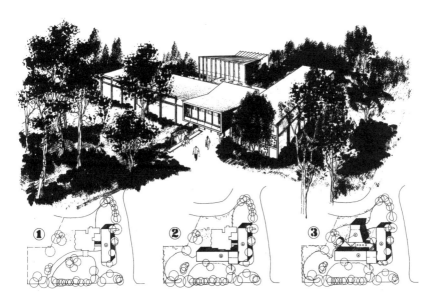

Three more proposals for the addition, *c.* 1956: "1" resembles the plan that would have saved the porte-cochère, while "3" would have entailed the destruction of the whole mansion. "2" is close to the plan for the Centennial Galleries as actually constructed, but without the north wing.
ART GALLERY OF GREATER VICTORIA ARCHIVES

on CBC Radio, and after hearing it, Mrs. Graham, who was living in Victoria, telephoned her son in California to congratulate him—much to his surprise.[17]

Relocating to Victoria with Graham was his wife, Sylvia, whom he had married in 1946. She had a degree in architecture from McGill University but never practised, instead focusing on homemaking and motherhood. When her domestic responsibilities permitted, Sylvia enthusiastically supported the arts centre, arranging the Volunteer Committee's house tour, making cardboard storage boxes for works of art, and working as a docent until 2001.

Apart from his duties on Moss Street, Graham wrote a weekly arts column, "Art in Review," for the Victoria *Daily Times* from 1953 to 1954. Graham also authored articles on local cultural and environmental topics and on international affairs. For example, in 1960, he urged Victoria architects to take a more imaginative approach toward the style of new buildings.[18] He stayed on staff at the arts centre as director emeritus on a half-time basis until 1980. An artist in his own right, he resumed painting after retiring in 1973, creating works that delight in the rural landscape of the Saanich Peninsula.

When Graham began as curator, his salary was two hundred dollars a month, plus free accommodation in Gyppeswyk. In a letter from artist and arts centre board member Ina Uhthoff dated June 22, 1951, Graham learned that he and his wife could live in a "beautiful suite of rooms on the ground floor with its own bathroom. This would go with the job!" On July 19, 1951, board member Hildegarde Wyllie told Graham that Gyppeswyk had "several nice suites with bathroom all complete and the one on the ground floor can be made to lead directly into the kitchen."[19]

The Grahams were supposed to move into their suite of rooms when Sara Spencer vacated the mansion, but the latter had to delay her departure because her new home on Cadboro Bay Road was not yet ready. And so, Gyppeswyk's last Spencer resident invited the Grahams to be guests in her home until she finally

The Centennial Wing, from Moss Street, c. 1956: Clack, Clayton, and Pickstone's sketch of an addition, which was chosen by a panel of assessors and approved by the board of directors. Later expansion would take place to the south (left). Care was taken to preserve the Garry oaks.
ART GALLERY OF GREATER VICTORIA ARCHIVES

moved out on November 13, 1951—one week before Victoria Arts Centre opened.

As it turned out, while it was free accommodation, the Grahams' apartment was upstairs and not particularly "beautiful." Despite what they had been told, they ended up living in the small apartment previously occupied by Sara Spencer's cook, Ho, in the northwest corner of the second floor of the mansion.[20] It comprised a small sitting room, a bedroom, and a bathroom, but not, at first, a kitchen, so the Grahams had to go downstairs to cook their meals. The condition of the suite cannot have been ideal because the board felt compelled to make continual improvements to it, in order to "make the apartment liveable."[21] Plus, despite improvements to the wiring and heating, it was cold and draughty. When storms buffeted Gyppeswyk, exposed as it was on its picturesque slope, the wind whistled through the window frames, making the counterweights therein rattle.[22] The installation of an oil-powered furnace helped considerably, but eventually presented a fire hazard. (A later tenant, housekeeper

The Centennial Wing, as constructed, 1958: Starkly modern with a glassed-in passageway in place of the porte-cochère, but a structure suited to the functioning of a "Class A" art gallery. At this time, the library (the windows at the far right) was still intact. After 1974, it was gutted to become the gallery's shop. Further expansion in 1977 engulfed and transformed the new entrance.
ART GALLERY OF GREATER VICTORIA ARCHIVES

Helen Todd, complained that one wall in her living room became alarmingly hot whenever that furnace came on.)

The Grahams' lives at Gyppeswyk were complicated by the fact that, for security purposes, someone had to be on the premises at all times, which meant they could not attend social or professional functions together. (And, needless to say, they did not have the servants who had supported the lives of the Greens, the Spencers, the McInneses, and the Lotbinières!) As well, when an occasional exhibit featured especially valuable artworks, Graham felt obliged to sleep in the cloakroom near the front door—even after he and Sylvia moved out.

In 1952, Colin Graham told the arts centre board of directors that he and his wife would be leaving their small upstairs flat because they were expecting their first child and the apartment was too small for a family. Their move was also prompted by the fact that, since he lived on site, many assumed the curator was always on call, a situation that was compromising his privacy and his health. In January 1953, therefore, the Grahams moved to a remodelled barn designed by John Di Castri on Nancy Hanks Street near Cedar Hill Cross Road.[23]

Making an Art Gallery

In 1957, Victoria arts critic Audrey St. Denys Johnson wrote that "one of the greatest assets of the gallery" was the "homely, informal atmosphere" the house exuded,[24] a quality Gyppeswyk still retains. Immediately upon its opening as the Victoria Arts Centre, the mansion bustled with a degree of activity it had rarely seen before. Between September 1951 and December 1952, twenty thousand visitors thronged its rooms and the halls of Gyppeswyk once again echoed with the voices of children, for three thousand of these visitors were young art students taking classes in the upstairs bedrooms.[25] Within a decade, the gallery had the largest ratio of members to population of any civic art museum in Canada. To augment its income, the main floor rooms were rented out for meetings, lectures, and live concerts. Films on art were also shown and concerts of recorded music could be attended. Theatre companies produced plays there[26] and a puppet show was staged in February 1957. The Women's Committee began to hold occasional supper dances, affairs of the kind Martha Worlock probably would have approved.[27] For example, in April 1956, sixty people sat down to a buffet dinner in the Spencer and Kearley Galleries (formerly the drawing and dining rooms).

But how suitable was Gyppeswyk for use as an art museum or gallery? Precedents abound for the use of an older mansion as the heart of a civic art gallery. In St. Catharines, Ontario, for example, Rodman Hall, built in 1856 by Thomas Rodman Merritt, became that city's arts centre in 1960. An ugly addition was built onto the side of the mansion, and later a more sympathetic one was added to the rear, but the front facade remains unchanged. Toronto's The Grange, built in 1817, became an art museum in 1911; closer to Victoria, Burnaby's art gallery is housed in Fairacres, the 1911 neo-Tudor home of Henry and Grace Ceperley.

In Victoria, however, the rooms of what people were by then calling the Spencer Mansion were proving to be ill adapted to the exhibition of most works of art—despite Governor General Vincent

Massey having praised the "suitability of the building to the needs of a gallery."[28] Colin Graham's comments at the formal opening may have been more prescient: "I was impressed with the building and intrigued with the problem of turning the house into a gallery."[29]

Indeed, a problem did exist. Although the arts centre's board of directors had noted in 1951 that the house was conveniently located near certain schools, the mansion's site was removed from tourist and cultural attractions and was off the beaten track even for many native to Victoria. Worse, as Willard Ireland had warned, the provincial archives would not lend the arts centre any works by Emily Carr, nor would most other lending institutions part even temporarily with any works because the "highly combustible" Gyppeswyk was not fireproof. In fact, Colin Graham frankly expressed relief that the nearby Yates Street fire hall was still in operation in the early 1950s.[30] It seemed the mansion would remain a "Class B" gallery until improvements were made. Major Cuthbert Holmes, an early supporter of the art gallery project, suggested the mansion be used for a maximum of twenty years before an addition was built or a completely new site was chosen. At one point in 1952, Mayor Harrison suggested that the arts centre move to Craigdarroch Castle.[31] Some people also expressed the view that Gyppeswyk's location in the Rockland district suggested the house was an exclusive playground for the affluent, a misconception that was reinforced by a local writer's description of the house as having "an air of butlers, candlelight and elegance."[32] (Moving the art gallery to a more central location downtown has been discussed repeatedly over the years. One can only speculate as to the fate of Gyppeswyk should the gallery move elsewhere.) Certainly by the mid-1950s, the fabric of the house needed to change to accommodate its new functions. The collection was growing, the number of functions was increasing, and storage space was increasingly unsuitable. Accordingly, Colin Graham and the arts centre board of directors set about making improvements.

DISCREET ALTERATIONS

If the Greens or the Spencers could walk into their family home today, they would recognize the foyer, the dining room, and perhaps the drawing room, but some of the changes to the mansion's interior, especially to the upstairs bedrooms, might leave them disoriented. Alterations to Gyppeswyk, however, were necessary. Despite its elegant exterior and well-preserved interior, the mansion had not been designed as a public building, much less as an art museum. In 1951, it was an old house by Victoria standards and there were parts that needed updating if it was to be used for any modern purpose. Only some of the most significant changes will be noted here. Most of these updates were, as the arts centre's monthly bulletin declared, "discreet."[1] However, one important alteration was not.

Paramount among the updates was improving the house's electrical system, which began after a visit from the fire marshal in early 1952. But in March 1957, the board of directors was informed of the "serious state of the wiring in the art gallery, which will not in its present condition pass the electrical inspector's requirements."[2] More improvement was required.

By the mid-1970s, a burglar alarm, a sprinkler system, and smoke sensors had been installed throughout the wooden building. Two steel fire escapes had been added to the mansion's north facade. Eventually the efficient but more aesthetically pleasing glassed-in

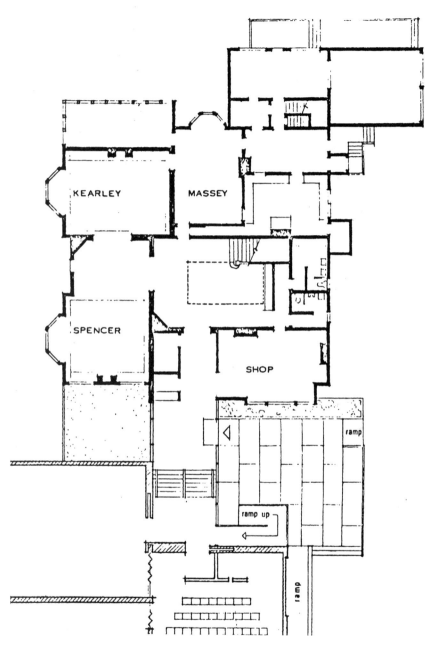

The main floor of Gyppeswyk, c. 1977: The Centennial and Ker Galleries (at the bottom of the map) had been added (1958). The library had become the shop (1974), public washrooms had been added to the foyer, and the side entrance and back door were still adjacent to the garage (upper right).

emergency staircase was also added. Because this new feature limited the effectiveness of the art nouveau window above the grand staircase, fluorescent lighting was installed to illuminate the window, highlighting its design and colours.

The look of the walls in the three main rooms changed frequently. Between July and November 1951, the walls of the drawing and morning rooms were painted white and fitted with one hundred and thirty yards of drapes and burlap broadcloth to make picture-hanging easier. The dining room walls were painted ivory and the woodwork grey. In time, these rooms were outfitted with display cases and plinths. In 1955, the walls of the upstairs gallery were also covered with burlap. In the mid-1970s, the walls in the drawing, morning, and dining rooms were covered with an exuberant sunflower-patterned wallpaper, ostensibly based on a William Morris pattern. Fluorescent lights were installed in the ceilings and the drawing room windows were fitted with sun blinds to protect the exhibits. By 1952, antique furniture had been provided for the foyer. Two public bathrooms were built on the north side of the building, off the foyer (beneath the stairs and the art nouveau window). Each had a coloured glass window with a lotus pattern. Later, a vertical-slatted wooden screen was added to separate the entry to these facilities from the rest of the foyer where lounge couches were installed. (These were removed in 1976 and replaced with chairs and tables.) Meanwhile, the library became the meeting room for the board of directors. It was also occasionally rented out for meetings of community groups. A carpenter's shop was fitted up in the basement, which was partly used for crating and uncrating travelling exhibits.

Painters, potters, and weavers were provided with studios in the second-floor bedrooms. In 1956, the board discussed the possibility of using the attic for painting and crafts classes. This would have required new stairs and better lighting, but the heating was believed to be sufficient. In the end, the plan had to be dropped because of the associated costs and because the fire marshal would

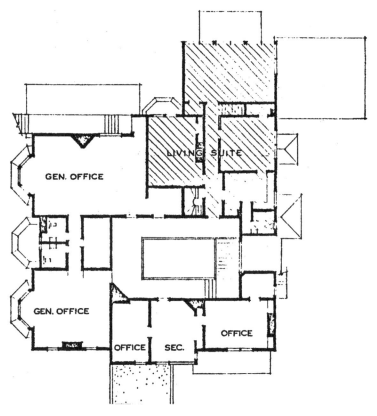

The second floor of Gyppeswyk, *c.* 1977: The porte-cochère was gone, but the servants' spiral staircase was still in place. At this time the bedrooms had long been in use as offices, but the living suite (the hatched area) was also about to be converted into offices. To the left of the corridor was the living room; to the right, the bedroom. The unhatched space attached to it was the bathroom. The largest space, over the laundry wing, was for general use.

ART GALLERY OF GREATER VICTORIA ARCHIVES

allow only twelve people in the attic at one time.[3] By 1973, the board was making new plans to renovate the attic so it could be used to house offices and collections when it learned the space could not be used for human occupancy under the building code. The attic has since become the Art Gallery of Greater Victoria's archive and storage space. (At the time of writing, the only regular activity in these rooms is that of a dedicated volunteer archivist and some panicked silverfish.)

In 1953, the arts centre's Women's Committee paid for new floors to be laid in the Kearley and Massey Galleries. The former dining and morning rooms received parquet and linoleum floors, respectively. The committee also installed a modern kitchen and opened a tearoom in the conservatory in 1959, but, because it lacked heating, they settled for using the morning room (later the Massey Gallery). The kitchen was improved in 1978, when the morning room became a café that thrived under professional management.

Any older house is bound to have certain problems and this was the case with Gyppeswyk. Besides the updates required to the electrical system, the drains in the basement began backing up in 1956 and required attention. The old furnace was removed in 1958 and replaced with one fuelled by oil instead of coal. The tall, elegant chimneys were also becoming dilapidated and there was talk of removing them in 1958, before they were eventually repaired in 1968. (They have since been repaired again as well as stabilized.) In 1980, dry rot was discovered in the garden facade porch that necessitated repair.

Unfortunately, improving how the house functioned as an art gallery involved some damage to Gyppeswyk's interior. In April 1974, the library was gutted so that a gift shop could be installed. Like the decision to paint over the Lincrusta-Walton wainscotting of the dining room, this move was questionable. On the other hand, as we have seen, some structural decay had occurred before, as well as after, the arts centre moved in. The loss of some valuable features, therefore, may have been inevitable, especially given financial constraints. For instance, the ornate fireplaces proved problematic as their flues were in poor shape and no longer operational. The Minton tiles and the woodwork were removed from most of the fireplaces, although the practical rationale for doing so is not clear. (Some of the tiles went into storage; others simply disappeared.) With the exception of the hearths in the foyer and on the upstairs landing, plain mantelpieces eventually replaced the ornate woodwork of the originals, so that useless gaping holes remain as reminders of their former function. (The woodwork on the fireplace in the morning room was preserved but was painted white. In the northeast bedroom on the second floor, a classical mantelpiece was allowed to stand.) At some point during renovations, the chandelier that now hangs in the dining room—where it is assumed it originally hung—became affixed to the lower newel post of the grand staircase, upside down!

Occasionally, renovations to Gyppeswyk's rooms were carried out to allow use of them for essential art gallery services. During renovations in 1974, for example, the dining and morning rooms were used as office space. This involved the further loss of some detail and decorative architectural features. The safety of both the public and the gallery staff also had to be considered. In 1972, a new interior staircase was constructed on the west side of the house, between the laundry wing and the older part of the mansion. In 1988, the fire protection systems and emergency exits were again renovated and upgraded, and the glassed-in emergency staircase was added to the north facade.

Over the years, the art gallery's several directors and boards of directors have not been insensitive to Gyppeswyk's historical or heritage value. In fact, in 1969, they discussed the "advisability of having part of the Spencer Mansion furnished in period style for the summer months," reasoning that this would be a "significant tourist attraction."[4] Throughout 1974, the board expressed a wish to "renovate" the mansion and "to refurbish it as closely as possible to its original form." They felt the ground floor should be "brought back to its original decor."[5] In that year, then-Director Richard Simmins received a grant from the National Museums of Canada for the restoration of the mansion. Unfortunately, no one seems to have had a clear idea of what this would entail. Nineteenth-century paintings, however, were hung in the three main rooms, which were returned to their original appearance—at least as far as the wall covering was concerned. This restoration project also saw the application of the aforementioned sunflower wallpaper. Five years later, another director, Roger Boulet, expressed what others must have felt. The "restoration," he said, was "a disaster, an interior designer's nightmare."[6] His plan was to make

The morning room, as a temporary office: Before the construction of the new wings (in and after 1958), and as the art gallery's functions grew in success and size, Gyppeswyk's formal rooms occasionally had to serve as office space. A fireplace, painted white, serves as a curious backdrop to a desk, filing cabinet, and other miscellaneous practical objects. Compare this to the earlier view of the same room with Graham and students on page 21.

ART GALLERY OF GREATER VICTORIA ARCHIVES

the Spencer Gallery into a typical Victorian drawing room, to be managed by the gallery's decorative arts curator. He considered a similar treatment for the Kearley and Massey Galleries. Little was accomplished at this time, however, although the sunflowers disappeared. By the 1990s, the walls of the Spencer Gallery had assumed a lilac colour, with matching tiles around the fireplaces, but this decorative element did not survive into the twenty-first century.

Outdoors, the lawns and gardens surrounding Gyppeswyk posed another problem. In 1951, one Victoria resident suggested the grounds become "a specialized botanical English landscape garden," appropriate to the background of the mansion's original owners and attractive to tourists.[7] This was not done, and neglect, leading to deterioration, set in, leaving "what was once a beautiful garden in a deplorable condition,"

The Japanese Garden, seen from Gyppeswyk's attic, 2011: Appropriately secluded and facing the mansion's south facade, with the ubiquitous Garry oaks. Established in 1977, it reflects the fine Asian collection in the modern wing (to the left).

PETER REID

according to a 1952 *Times* letter writer.[8] City Council had reneged on its commitment to maintain the grounds. With the Governor General's visit to formally open the arts centre planned for October 15, 1952, J. Ronald Grant, president of the arts centre board, appealed desperately to the mayor and the council on September 17 for some men and equipment to remedy the garden's "serious state of disrepair."[9] The records show no further pleas for help; presumably the City authorities were shamed into action.

In 1953, the resident janitor, Alec Burns, took charge, at least, of cutting the grass. He was occasionally assisted by men from Neon Products of Western Canada Ltd. who volunteered their time. The gardens continued to be untidy, however, and even the Spencers were concerned. In April 1963, Mrs. Will Spencer and others suggested hiring a professional gardener to refurbish the grounds. Nothing came of this plan, and by October of that year, "morning glory [was] getting a hold in the front garden."[10] Probably due to lack of funds, once again little was accomplished. In 1966, the board expressed concern over the state of the grounds in the summer months, and so, in 1967, boys from Central Junior High School were paid at intervals to clean the grounds. Some landscaping on the Moss Street side was done in 1972.

Finally, in 1974, a Local Initiatives Program grant allowed for the garden fronting the south facade to be redesigned by Harold Spence-Sales, an architect and town planner. Then in 1977, Margaret Ely and a group of volunteers transformed it into a Japanese garden. For a while, community service workers maintained the area. A Shinto shrine was installed in 1986. The Greens might have been surprised at this alien intrusion on their property, but perhaps the Spencers would have been pleased—Japanese gardens (such as the one on the Gorge waterway) had become popular during their occupancy of Gyppeswyk. (Volunteers maintain the area today.)

Despite the improvements, many supporters of the arts centre still believed Gyppeswyk was an unsatisfactory—and therefore only temporary—solution to Victoria's need for a technologically efficient exhibition space for works of art. A modern addition to the mansion would have to be built.

Construction of the Centennial Wing

In 1955, the Victoria Rotary Club, with the support of the Architectural Institute of BC, volunteered to sponsor an architectural competition for a suitable plan. When announcing the contest, the arts centre's board of directors stipulated that the addition must be built on the north side of Gyppeswyk, in order to preserve the driveway and porte-cochère, and that it should be erected at a safe distance from the mansion so that it would not be damaged in a possible fire. The directors hoped that a covered walkway leading from the mansion to the new wing would be built and that a storage area would be constructed adjacent to the garage. The "Requirements" also envisaged another wing to be built on the south side of the mansion in the future. (The latter plan survived until at least 1962, after the Centennial and Ker rooms were added, and conceived what would become the Founders Gallery [1970], connecting this annex and enclosing a sculpture garden.)

The conditions for the competition were announced in January 1956. In March of that year, the jury of assessors, which included Colin Graham, awarded first prize to the Victoria firm of Clack, Clayton, and Pickstone, who had submitted plans for not only a north wing but also an east wing (i.e., on the front facade of the mansion). In awarding first prize, said the assessors, "the relation of the new building to the existing is . . . well balanced and harmonious."[11] The architects were invited to proceed with final sketch plans.

By October 1956, Clack, Clayton, and Pickstone had produced a model of the proposed addition, which was exhibited in Gyppeswyk. The final plans had been revised to eliminate the north wing. In doing so, they explained the need for a parking lot on the north side of the building rather than on the east side, where it might be awkward. This north-side parking lot would use an area screened by trees, making it a more aesthetically pleasing site than in front of the mansion. Another consideration was that access to the north wing would have been unsuitably far, they believed, from main entrance to the mansion.

The competition winners and the judges may have taken into consideration other matters too. If a new wing had been added to the north facade, access to the foyer from this new wing might have been impeded by the grand staircase, whose removal would have been a greater loss than the loss of the porte-cochère, which ensued. Moreover, building to the north might have entailed removing or at least truncating the necessary steel fire escapes that had been added to the north facade in the early 1950s. Finally, there was no room to the west, since the Gyppeswyk property directly slopes sharply down to Pentrelew Place. Presumably, the board agreed with the addition as proposed by Clack, Clayton, and Pickstone, thus abandoning the north wing project and accepting the loss of the porte-cochère and the driveway.[12] Records of the board's deliberations at this time are sparse, but discussions apparently ensued in November 1956, resulting in this decision.

Apparently the board of directors gave considerable attention to the siting and appearance of the addition. In the spring of 1957, the board's secretary noted that "all items bought in by the curator, the Building Design and Building Construction Committees are being thoroughly thrashed out." Further discussions with the architects were held in the early fall until the board finally put the plan out to public tender in October 1957. In December, M.P. Paine and Co. received the contract.

Throughout the planning process, concern was expressed for the survival of the Garry oaks trees that were part of the semi-rural landscape that had originally attracted the Greens to Rockland and had inspired the Spencers to name the house "under the oaks." As it turned out, only eight of the seventy-five trees on the property had to be sacrificed to make room for the addition.[13] During construction, the builders set up protection around the remaining oaks to prevent damage to their trunks and roots—a level of concern upheld when later additions were made. (During construction of the Pollard Gallery in 1977, for example, two hundred and fifty dollars was spent on guy wires to brace and support one endangered oak tree.)

In September 1958, the modern annex was opened, connected with Gyppeswyk by a glassed-in walkway in place of the mansion's porte-cochère. The addition comprised two adjoining exhibition halls, called the North and South Centennial Galleries in celebration of British Columbia's centennial. The structure cost seventy-five thousand dollars and—most important—was fireproof. A basement vault for the preparation and storing of art was also included. The arts centre now had a "Class A" structure and could thus host travelling exhibits from the National Gallery and other lending institutions.[14] After its completion, Anthony Emery, president of the board of directors, wrote to Roderick Clack to report that "the gallery directors were delighted with the design"[15] of the new wing.

Despite the technical modernity gained by the expanded arts centre, now known as the Art Gallery of Greater Victoria, some locals believed the addition to be problematic. Judge Herbert Davey, the gallery's neighbour to the south, said he found it "disappointingly unattractive."[16] Others saw problems with its aesthetic relationship to Gyppeswyk, with one historian calling the addition "unsympathetic."[17] For some heritage conservationists, the expansion seemed "awkward" and the new galleries "tacked on."[18] On the other hand, for a few observers, no problem existed. For example, historian Robin Ward believed that the two linked structures "co-exist[ed] in honest architectural harmony."[19] Whether or not one approves of the look of the newer structures is a matter of taste and opinion. It is indisputable, however, that the architectural integrity of Gyppeswyk was seriously damaged by the construction of the Centennial Galleries, though few Victoria residents were concerned about it at the time.

The Past is Past

In 1935, Emily Carr was contemptuous of the local Art Historical Society and its concern over the preservation of "old buildings," writing that "the needs of today are pressing" and adding that "the past is past."[20] When someone as sensitive and intelligent as one of Canada's leading artists—who was trying to preserve a record of the art and architecture of First Nations—could so peremptorily dismiss the preservation of what we now value as heritage architecture, it should come as no surprise that Gyppeswyk's facade was ruined just twenty years later—and during more prosperous times.

In the 1950s, Canadians did not value their architectural heritage as much as they do now. At the time, it must have seemed more important to ensure the art gallery looked modern and was technologically up-to-date, than worry if the existing structure and new addition were harmoniously linked in style or if the facade of a valuable Victorian mansion was damaged.

If we consider the development of heritage awareness in Victoria, the destruction of Gyppeswyk's facade was part of a trend during the post-war boom era. For example, the Creases' Pentrelew, nearby on Fort Street, was demolished, and even more significant structures came under threat in the 1940s and '50s. City Hall, which was designed by John Teague and opened in 1878, was put up for sale in 1946. A developer planned to demolish it, intending to replace it with a department store. This project came to nothing, but the building was threatened again in 1957 by new plans to tear it down. (Clearly the landmark survived in spite of these threats.) Significantly, when the gallery's Women's Committee tried in 1958 to include "old historical homes" in their annual fundraising house tour, they found that none were "available." They reasoned this was because such homes were either unsympathetically renovated or inhabited by "old people" who did not want to be disturbed by tours.[21] From this perspective, the survival of even a mutilated Gyppeswyk seems almost miraculous.

As works of modern architecture, the new additions were, and still are, inoffensive. (The original Centennial Wings have been subsumed in the later additions.) But absolutely no congruity of architectural style between the old and new structures exists, and the removal of the porte-cochère amounted to cutting off the nose of a beautiful face. Although Colin Graham, in his Curator's Report to the Annual Meeting in 1956, declared, "At the present time we are giving a great deal of thought to the siting of the [new] wing,"[22] no public criticism around the removal of this organic piece of Gyppeswyk's body was heard. Furthermore, no remarks concerning the port-cochère can be found in the specifications in the original contract with the builder. As for the Spencer family, and Sara Spencer in particular, the records do not include their reaction to the removal of this distinguishing feature of their family home. The board of directors in the years 1955–1958 included at least three architects, one photographer, and several artists, all people who might have been sensitive to the need to retain the integrity of a beautiful building. The records, however, do not contain objections from any of them to the removal of the porte-cochère. The only contemporary comment on the subject comes from John Bertram Green, the youngest son of Alexander and Theophila Green, who visited the family home in 1958 and remarked, "it is too bad the entrance to the old house has been torn down."[23]

In any case, while construction was underway, Gyppeswyk remained open as a functioning art gallery. During this period, and while all sorts of other renovations were going on, the mansion was never vandalized nor did it burn down, which was due, at least in part, to a small cadre of janitors, caretakers, and cleaners who maintained the house—and even lived in it—for twenty years.

Unsung Heroes

Although Gyppeswyk became a public institution in 1951, it remained a residence for certain people. After Colin and Sylvia Graham moved out, but still during Colin's tenure as director, others made the house their home. These individuals, largely unremembered today, should be honoured for their role in keeping Gyppeswyk safe from fire, vermin, and burglary. Underpaid, working long hours, and living in inadequate accommodation, but often dedicated and loyal, most of them shared Colin Graham's commitment and enthusiasm for the house and the arts centre it housed, and went the extra mile to maintain the mansion.

In 1951, a janitor was hired to work on the evenings when meetings or other occasions were held in Gyppeswyk. When the Grahams vacated the upstairs apartment, a live-in cleaning person and a handyman/janitor were deemed necessary. As a result, Mr. and Mrs. Robert W. Rhodes moved into the upstairs flat in 1953. The suite was unfurnished and, like the Grahams, the Rhodes had to use the kitchen on the main floor. The young couple paid rent to the arts centre but also received a nominal monthly salary. Their tenure was brief and, for reasons that are unclear, they were asked to resign and move out.

The Rhodes were succeeded by Noel and Isabella Davis. Noel, who was "steady and very dependable,"[24] had been a cook at University School and knew some carpentry. He did maintenance jobs and helped with the crating and uncrating of travelling exhibits, which usually took place in the basement or garage. Isabella kept the mansion clean. However, again for unclear reasons, the Davises were given notice to vacate the upstairs suite in January 1955. Noel continued to work in Gyppeswyk from time to time as a security guard and part-time carpenter. For example, he helped produce the display cases for the Drury Gallery that were added in 1970.

A new housekeeper, Mary Silverthorne, a widow originally from Vancouver, moved into the caretakers' quarters in February 1955 and took over light housekeeping duties in exchange for ten dollars a month. Despite the fact that she had to always be on the premises after closing time so as not to leave the galleries unattended, she volunteered in the Tea Room that operated in the Massey Gallery until at least 1988 and did, in Colin Graham's words, "a really magnificent job" on one of the Women's Committee's rummage sales.[25] In 1955, when the health of then-resident janitor Alec Burns, who had been living in the basement room, began to fail, Mary's suite was suitably divided to provide accommodation for him. (Burns, however, soon resigned and moved out.) A kitchen was finally installed upstairs in 1957, and the bathroom refurbished.

In 1958, James and Helen Todd took up residence in the upstairs suite as live-in caretakers, becoming "familiar and much-liked personalities."[26] James helped maintain the lawns and voluntarily created a garden in the area now covered by the parking lot. He continued to serve as a security guard until failing health compelled him to resign. After his death, donations from friends enabled the gallery to purchase three works of art in his memory. His wife, Helen, served as housekeeper and worked occasionally at the reception desk until she died in 1971. A dynamo, she repainted the children's and adult art studies upstairs and the washrooms downstairs. She was described as "a character" and "very Scottish."[27] Helen was a favourite with the Grahams' sons and treated them to cookies. She also dressed very well, purchasing used clothes at the Women's Committee "Classy Cast-Offs" sales. Her popularity at Gyppeswyk was shown by the memorial fund established in her name. Because she had been interested in Asian art, monies from the fund were used to purchase rare Japanese pottery jars. The Todds were the last couple to make Gyppeswyk their home. In 1976, James Todd, then a widower, was asked to vacate the upstairs suite. Their small apartment was converted into offices, one of which—the suite's original bathroom—still has its white wainscotting.

Well into the 1960s, it was necessary for insurance purposes to have someone in residence in the mansion twenty-four hours a day. The caretaker(s) living upstairs and the custodian staying in the basement had to arrange for one of them to always be on site. In 1962, Helen Todd expressed a plaintive wish: "to get out sometimes in the evenings."[28] Upon considering her case, the board decided that she and resident janitor Erik Binas should be allowed to call on the Canadian Corps of Commissionaires when they both wanted to leave the premises. But they had to let Colin Graham know if they were going to be out for more than an hour and give one day's notice if they were going to be gone overnight. On occasions when one or the other was left in charge, they were "permitted to leave the premises for fifteen minutes in order to get provisions."[29] Given these strictures, their dedication seems even more remarkable.

The simple, low-ceilinged basement room vacated in 1951 by the Spencers' servant Sam was the residence of a series of guards, handymen, and janitors. They were paid ten dollars a month and received free accommodation—at least at first. These insalubrious, unfurnished quarters came with a hot plate but not much else. The board's minutes indicate that pensioners were preferred for this position, but the preference entailed its own disadvantage. The first of these solitary caretakers was George Rutley. He was hired in 1952 but died soon after, on October 5th of that year. Apparently his death was a great loss to the arts centre because the board recorded that he had come "to occupy a special place in the esteem and affection of all who worked or became acquainted with him."[30]

Another retiree succeeded Rutley: James McDonald was hired on a full-time basis at ten dollars a month in October 1952. McDonald soon resigned and was replaced in 1953 first by Herbert Courtnall and very soon afterwards by Alec Burns, who had been hired as a daytime janitor in 1951. On one occasion, Burns petitioned the board to be allowed to paint his dreary accommodations, but the records do not suggest whether or not his petition was granted. In the spring of 1954, he took on maintenance of the grounds, after the City reneged on this matter, for which he was paid an extra twelve dollars a month. When Burns was hospitalized for eye surgery, the board granted him a leave of absence with pay. As noted above, in late 1955, he was allowed to move into the newly subdivided apartment upstairs. Burns, like most of these men, was an elderly pensioner and was hard of hearing so his usefulness in case of intruders or calamities at night was limited. Still, Colin Graham called him "a devoted servant to the gallery." Even as his health deteriorated, the board continued to require his "invaluable" services while encouraging him to "ease up."[31]

When Burns moved upstairs, the basement room's new tenant was seventy-one-year-old Wellington Gable, who was described as a "packer" or "assistant to the curator." Gable's work helping Burns pack and crate artworks was not satisfactory, so in 1955 he was replaced briefly by R.H. Cochrane, a retired teamster.

In September 1955, a young Dane named Erik Binas, who had been a patcher with BC Forest Products, moved into the basement suite and assumed the duties of handyman and janitor. As an "assistant" to Director Colin Graham, he was loyal and co-operative, and praised for his "services and help far above and beyond the call of duty."[32] Probably for this reason, in the spring of 1958, the board sponsored him to be trained as a museum technician at the Vancouver Art Gallery.

In November 1961, the board approved five weeks of sick leave and sent him flowers in the hospital. Binas was also permitted an unusual five-week holiday in 1963. He was employed by the Art Gallery of Greater Victoria and lived in Gyppeswyk until 1965, after which he went on to work at the Seattle Art Museum as well as in California.

Frederick Potter, who had been a caretaker at the nearby Victoria Truth Centre (on the former site of the Crease family home) and a part-time guard at the art gallery, replaced Binas as caretaker and packer, living in the basement flat until December 1966. When Potter died in 1968, the gallery remembered him as "conscientious" and "friendly." [33]

For the convenience of the janitors, Helen Todd had donated a small plug-in stove to embellish the cellar apartment. Around the same time, the board discussed the advisability of installing storm windows and an electric heater in the vacated suite "to make it habitable." [34]

George Carter succeeded Potter in both the basement suite and the custodial duties. A retired Alberta farmer, he was fascinated by the art on display and freely gave of his opinions. Dedicated and efficient, he was, however, reluctant to shave regularly. One day, a volunteer receptionist approached Colin Graham, convinced that "there's a thug in the gallery . . . frightful to look at!" Colin assured her the apparition was quite harmless. [35] Like Binas, Carter worked as a framer and crater of the works of art. He was the last person to inhabit the basement apartment, leaving in 1976.

These people, today almost forgotten, helped to preserve much of Gyppeswyk's integrity. Thanks in part to them, the mansion, although damaged, survives today and bustles with life as a hub for Victoria's artists and artistic activity. Of course, the Greens and the Spencers might not approve of the changes made to their home. Both its interior and its exterior have been altered and may be altered further still; any further changes, we hope, will be discreet.

INTO THE TWENTY-FIRST CENTURY

We may nostalgically regret the fact that Gyppeswyk is no longer a home, that we cannot smell old-fashioned cooking coming from the kitchen, nor hear the voices of children playing in the upstairs bedrooms, nor eavesdrop on quiet soirées in the drawing room. On the other hand, it is no longer painted a bland white, nor does it stand modestly as a mere annex to the more boldly modern galleries built in the 1950s and 1970s. Instead, Gyppeswyk now firmly asserts its identity as an impressive, handsome, earth-toned villa, redolent with Victoria's past—and part of its potential future.

Gyppeswyk's three main-floor rooms underwent much alteration in the first two decades of their use as exhibition spaces. On several occasions, the board expressed a desire to restore these rooms to their late-Victorian appearance; however, this ultimately led to the ill-advised restoration of the dining and drawing rooms. Individual acts of rehabilitation elsewhere in the house were also undertaken. In 1968, for example, there was talk of installing an available chandelier in the Tea Room. It must have been a nineteenth-century fixture because the board decided that if it was not "suitable" it would be purchased by a collector.[1] Today, the ceiling rosette surrounding the outlet for a light fixture is extant, but there is no chandelier. By the early 1970s, this room was furnished with tables and chairs reminiscent of the nineteenth century. The Women's Committee even advertised for a silver tea service and an oak side table to complete the atmosphere of the Tea Room. (It operated in the former morning room, which has since been renamed the Massey Gallery and is dedicated today to children's and local artists' work).

By 1999, only the foyer, with its beautiful woodwork, was intact—as it is today. On the walls, large paintings by local artist Sophie Pemberton document the lifestyle of families similar to the Greens and the Spencers. The fireplace is still a focus of attention as visitors enter the house. A large dollhouse records in miniature the furnishings and decor of a house like Gyppeswyk a century ago.

By the end of the 1990s, however, constructive change was coming. The dining room, now the Kearley Gallery, named for Mark Kearley, an early local supporter of the art gallery, was "sympathetically redesigned"[2] in 1999 by Stuart Stark, a heritage restoration architect. The gilded brass chandelier that graces the ceiling of the dining room was found on the lower newel post of the grand staircase. It was returned to its original place minus the chains that used to decorate it as swags and with new etched-glass shades. The wallpaper and plasterwork in this room were also restored, and the fireplace tiles are new. As in the foyer, the paintings on the walls reflect the taste and lifestyle of the late-nineteenth century. The Kearley Gallery is the most fully restored of all the main-floor spaces. Nowadays, the former dining room is the scene of enthusiastic meetings of dedicated docents and volunteers, as well as more relaxed receptions. In the drawing room, the ceiling has been partly restored. This space, which has been the scene of dramatic presentations as well as receptions, lectures, concerts, and even weddings, is embellished with paintings—mostly rural nineteenth-century scenes—that recall some of the ideals of our great-grandfathers. The exterior door leads to the beautiful Japanese Garden and the stunning Shinto shrine. In the former morning room, now known as the Massey Gallery, the building manager stripped the white paint from the fireplace around 2008, exposing its intricate woodwork and tiles.

Further traces of Gyppeswyk's former elegance remain upstairs, unavoidably concealed from the public. For instance, on the landing of the second floor, in the southeast corner, an original fireplace is intact, with its ornate woodwork and tiles. Similarly, the board room on the second floor is embellished with a door that features a large, coloured glass window, which may have been a part of the original house. The bedrooms still serve as offices (now overcrowded), as well as a library. There is an archive in the attic. The rooftop belvedere, which had suffered water damage, was repaired in 1990. In 2004, the Palladian windows of the attic floor were reconstructed.

By 2004, Gyppeswyk's exterior had been painted and repainted many times. From at least 1917 to about 1960, the walls were painted a greyish-white with a lighter trim. In 1975, the mansion was painted cream with a white trim, ostensibly to coordinate with the brick chosen for the new Pollard Gallery. By 2004, the exterior had again become a bleak, institutional black, grey, and white. However, that summer, Stuart Stark restored the house's original colours. After peeling away fifteen layers of paint, he ascertained that the mansion's original exterior colours were dark oxide red, dark green, and pale salmon. New versions of these shades were developed and christened "Spencer Red," "Gyppeswyk Green," and "Moss Street Coral." The roof was stained the same red as the trim. In places where they had decayed, the cedar shingles were repaired, and the chimneys were earthquake-proofed and re-pointed. An anonymous donor paid for the painting and roof repairs. The new colours make the mansion look more imposing—and would certainly please Alexander and Theophila Green.

Unfortunately, because of the loss of the porte-cochère and the installation of the glass-enclosed staircase on the north side, the mansion cannot be designated a heritage structure. On the other hand, the integrity of the house is more secure because the fire and theft protection systems are modern and guarantee the security of the house as far as humanly possible. Today, the mansion teems with more activity than it ever saw in its life as a mere residence. The parking lot is often so full that patrons and visitors have to park on nearby streets. Events such as the Art Gallery of Greater Victoria's annual "Paint-In" on Moss Street, for example, lure many in to admire the mansion, including people who never knew it was there.

This book has told the story of a house and the people who made it their home. Although Gyppeswyk has served as Victoria's art gallery for the last sixty years, men, women, and children inhabited Gyppeswyk for its first sixty years. Alexander Green's residency was truncated by illness and death, but his widow, Theophila, and her children, although their finances were troubled, continued, with a brief absence, to call it home until 1899. For several years, they shared the house with Frederick and Martha Worlock and their children, at a time when presumably kinship trumped overcrowding. Thomas and Martha McInnes scarcely had time to enjoy the mansion as political turmoil clouded their residency. Henri and Margaretta Joly de Lotbinière brought a touch of glamour to the house, especially with the royal banquet in 1901. David and Emma Spencer enjoyed Gyppeswyk for longer than any other residents, he until his death in 1920 and she until hers in 1934. Three Spencer sisters lived on in the home until finally Sara, having outlived her sisters, donated the house to the City of Victoria for use as an art gallery, so that we tend to refer to the building, somewhat incorrectly, as the Spencer Mansion. Colin and Sylvia Graham, both as residents for a brief time, and he as curator/director and she as a volunteer, also helped preserve Gyppeswyk. As well, several resident caretakers took care of the mansion in their own way, so that it never succumbed to fire or serious decay.

Many of these people both patronized and practised the arts, especially music, so that it is perhaps fitting that the house has enjoyed more than half a century as a showplace for the arts. Whether it's called Gyppeswyk, the Spencer Mansion, or Llan Derwen, the house endures, not only as a historical document, but also as a place full of potential for the future. As such, it belongs to all Victorians and seems to be guaranteed at least another century of vibrant life as a community centre. Surely, the Greens and the Spencers would approve.

The Guest List for the Banquet at Gyppeswyk in 1901

Duke and Duchess of Cornwall (later King George V and Queen Mary).

Prince Alexander of Teck (1874–1957), brother of Mary, duchess of Cornwall.

Lady Margaret Lygon (1874–1957), lady of the bedchamber to the duchess.

Lieutenant-Colonel Sir Derek William George Keppel (1863–1944), equerry to the duke from 1893 to 1910 and later master of the household from 1912 until 1936.

Honourable Mrs. Derek (Bridget Louisa) Keppel.

Lord Wenlock (1849–1912), lord of the bedchamber to the duke.

Lieutenant-Colonel Sir Arthur Bigge (1849–1931), the duke's private secretary.

Commander Sir Charles Leopold Henry Cust (1864–1939), equerry to the duke.

Sir John Anderson (1858–1918), of the British Colonial Office; later governor of Ceylon (Sri Lanka) and governor of Straits Settlements.

Sir Donald Mackenzie Wallace (1841–1919), correspondent for *The Times of London.*

Captain Sir Bryan Godfrey-Faussett (1863–1945), British naval officer; friend and aide-de-camp to the duke.

Captain Henry William, Viscount Crichton (1872–1914), aide-de-camp to the duke.

Major J.H. Orr, a military doctor.

Lieutenant of the Royal Horse Guards, John Innes-Ker, Duke of Roxburghe (1876–1932), a Scottish peer and another aide-de-camp to the duke.

Sir Henri Joly and Lady Joly de Lotbinière.

Captain Montague William Tyrwhitt-Drake (1830–1908), lawyer, judge, MLA, and mayor, 1876–77.

Miss Boswell, unidentifiable.

Mr. Robert B. Powell, private secretary to the lieutenant-governor. This man may also be the same R.B. Powell who was a tennis champion, and later secretary/treasurer of the North Pacific International Lawn Tennis Association (1904).

Rear Admiral Arthur Kennedy
Bickford (1844–1927),
commander of the British fleet at
Esquimalt, 1901–03, and his wife
and daughter.

Flag Lieutenant Knox, aide-de-camp
to Admiral Bickford.

Edward Cridge (1817–1913), bishop
of the Reformed Episcopal
Church, and his wife Mary
(1827–1905).

William Wilcox Perrin (1848–1934),
Anglican Bishop of British
Columbia, and his daughter,
unidentifiable.

Roman Catholic Bishop Bertram
Orth (1848–1931).

Edgar Dewdney (1835–1916),
former lieutenant-governor of
British Columbia, 1892–97, and
his wife, Jane.

Sir Hibbert Tupper (1835–1927),
Vancouver lawyer and federal
Conservative politician.

Senator William J. Macdonald, mayor,
1866–67, and his wife, Catherine.

Senator William Templeman
(1842–1914), Canadian Liberal
politician and managing editor
and owner of the Victoria *Daily
Times*, and his wife, Eva.

George W. Burbidge (1873–1908),
lawyer; later judge of the
Exchequer Court, forerunner of
the Federal Court of Canada.

George Anthony Walkem
(1834–1908), lawyer and former
premier, 1874–76, and his wife,
Sophia.

Paulus A. Irving, Supreme Court
judge, and his wife, Diana.

Joseph Martin (1852–1923), premier
in 1900, and his wife.

Henry Pering Pellew Crease
(1823–1905), politician, lawyer,
and judge; owner of Pentrelew
and a neighbour of Gyppeswyk.

Edward G. Prior (1853–1920),
businessman, engineer, and
premier, 1902–03, and his wife,
Genevieve.

Thomas Earle (1837–1911),
businessman and Conservative
MP representing Victoria, 1889–
1904, and his wife, Elizabeth.

David McEwen Eberts (1850–1924),
Attorney General, and his wife,
Mabel.

W.C. Wells, MLA for the North-East
riding of the Kootenay District.

Honourable T.D. Prentice (1861-?),
and his wife, Mabel.

John Herbert Turner (1834–1923),
businessman and premier,
1895–98, and his wife, Elizabeth.

Mrs. Laura Dunsmuir (1858–1937),
wife of Premier James Dunsmuir.

Lieutenant-Colonel A. Grant,
Royal Engineers (Work Point
Barracks), and his wife.

Lieutenant-Colonel G.T. Holmes, and his wife.

Lieutenant-Colonel Francis B. Gregory, Fifth Regiment (Work Point).

Charles Hayward (1839–1919), mayor of Victoria, 1900–1902.

Lady Mary Caroline Minto (1858–1940), wife of the Governor General, 1898–1908.

Sir Wilfrid Laurier (1841–1919), prime minister, 1896–1911.

Major Frederick Stanley Maude (1864–1917), Lord Minto's military secretary, and his wife.

Miss Grenfell, unidentifiable.

Captain Graham, unidentifiable.

NOTE: Although sixty-six guests are listed, Premier James Dunsmuir is not listed nor is Lord Minto (their wives, however, were present). Although the Governor General welcomed the royal pair in Ottawa and Montreal, he did not travel with them across the country. He reasoned that, at small government houses (such as Gyppeswyk), two vice-regal entourages—plus that of the duke and duchess—would make for overcrowding. As well, at special occasions, the provincial lieutenant-governors would want "to take the lead themselves." "I felt," he wrote, "that I might rather be in the way." So he sent his wife, Mary Caroline (Lady Minto). (Source: *Lord Minto's Canadian Papers . . . 1898–1904*, Toronto: The Champlain Society, Volume II, 1983, pp. 78ff.)

APPENDIX II

Details of Gyppeswyk's Design and Decor

A hearth tile: From one of Gyppeswyk's fireplaces, possibly the one in the drawing room. A typical geometric/floral design produced by Minton's in the 1870s. Such semi-abstract embellishments can still be seen in the hearth on the landing of the foyer.

ART GALLERY OF GREATER VICTORIA ARCHIVES SC 206 A-J

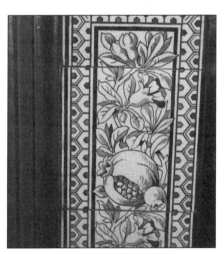

Tiles from the foyer fireplace: Although in Asia the pomegranate is a symbol of fertility and in Christianity it is a symbol of Jesus' suffering and resurrection, here it suggests abundance, an appropriate comment on the success of the Greens and the Spencers. It also appears in the wallpaper of the dining room.

ROBERT RATCLIFFE TAYLOR

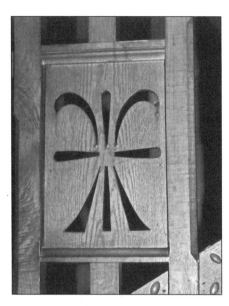

The grand staircase: Part of the Eastlake decoration of the balustrade. The abstract floral motif echoes the lines of the art nouveau window above the stairs.

PETER REID

Wallpaper in the dining room: Featuring a pattern inspired by the work of English designer and artist William Morris, this wall covering was applied during the sympathetic renovation of the room in 1999.

ROBERT RATCLIFFE TAYLOR

In the foyer: Detail of the north-facing window on the landing.
PETER REID

Exterior wall: Brackets supporting the eaves on the south facade.
PETER REID

Timeline

1834 Alexander Green born in Ixworth, Suffolk

1837 David Spencer born in St. Athan, Wales

1840 Theophila Turner Rainer (later Mrs. Green) born in Great Yarmouth, Norfolk

1842 Emma Lazenby (later Mrs. Spencer) born in Bubwith, East Yorkshire

1843 Fort Victoria constructed

1849 Crown Colony of Vancouver Island established

California Gold Rush began

1850 Frederick Hammett Worlock born in Bedminster, Bristol

1852 Martha Amelia Rainer (later Mrs. Worlock) born in Ipswich, Suffolk

1856–57 Fraser River Gold Rush began

Fort Victoria became provisioning centre for the gold rush

The "mainland" became a separate colony: British Columbia

Wells Fargo Express opened an agency in Victoria

1859 The Birdcages (original Legislative Buildings) built

1862 City of Victoria incorporated

Gas lighting of Victoria's streets introduced

Cariboo Gold Rush began

1863 David Spencer and Emma Lazenby arrived (separately) in Victoria

1864 Spencer opened his Reading Room and Library in Victoria

1866 Union of the colonies of Vancouver Island and British Columbia

Francis Garesche became Wells Fargo agent in Victoria

1867 Confederation of eastern British North America

1867 David Spencer and Emma Lazenby married in Victoria

1868 Spencer's Reading Room and Library burned

Victoria became the capital of BC

1871 British Columbia joined Confederation

1872 Alexander Green and Theophila Bird (née Rainer) married in Ipswich, Suffolk

1873 David Spencer, in partnership with William Denny, purchased the Victoria House

1873 Alexander and Theophila Green with their daughter Edna arrived in Victoria

1874 Alexander Green became an accountant with Wells Fargo in Victoria

1875 Francis Garesche drowned in the *Pacific* disaster
Water pipeline from Elk Lake to Victoria opened
1877 Formation of Garesche Green & Co.
1878 First telephone in Victoria
1879 David Spencer opened a dry goods store
1883 First electric street lights in Victoria
1885 First transcontinental train to Vancouver
1889 Construction of Gyppeswyk
1890 Electric streetcar service began in Victoria
1891 Alexander Green died
1892 Fredrick Worlock entered partnership with Theophila Green in Green Worlock & Co.
1894 Green Worlock & Co. collapsed
1896 Klondike Gold Rush began
1897 New Legislative Buildings opened
1897 Thomas Robert McInnes appointed lieutenant-governor
1899 Government House (Carey Castle) burned; McInnes and his wife, son, daughter-in-law, and grandson moved into Gyppeswyk
1900 Henri Joly de Lotbinière appointed lieutenant-governor (serving until 1906) and moved into Gyppeswyk with his wife
1901 Formal banquet at Gyppeswyk on the occasion of the visit of the Duke and Duchess of Cornwall
1899–1902 South African War
1903 David Spencer purchased Gyppeswyk
1905 Theophila Green died
1908 Empress Hotel opened
1910 The great fire in downtown Victoria
1914–1918 First World War
1917 Fiftieth wedding anniversary of David and Emma Spencer
1920 David Spencer died
1926 Frederick Worlock died
1934 Emma Spencer died
1939–1945 Second World War
1940 Martha Worlock died
1948 Eaton's took over David Spencer Limited
1951 Sara Spencer offered her family home to the Victoria Arts Centre for use as an art gallery
Appointment of Colin Graham as the first curator/director of the gallery at Gyppeswyk
First exhibition of paintings in Gyppeswyk
1952 Official opening of the Victoria Arts Centre (later the Art Gallery of Greater Victoria) at Gyppeswyk

ENDNOTES

INTRODUCTION

1 Willard Ireland, provincial archivist, in a lecture at Gyppeswyk, by then part of the Art Gallery of Greater Victoria, on December 19, 1959. (AGGV)

2 *Ibid.*

3 The book in your hands is not a history of the Art Gallery of Greater Victoria, although obviously the story of Gyppeswyk would be an integral part of such a chronicle (which I invite someone else to write!). This book ends *c.* 1977, after which time no one actually lived in the mansion; however, a brief afterword updates the story of the house itself to the beginning of the twenty-first century.

THE HOUSE THE GREENS BUILT

1 Edgar Fawcett, *Some Reminiscences of Old Victoria* (Toronto: Briggs, 1912), 28. Walking up the hill to school, he found "wild flowers . . . in profusion" (31).

2 Among British immigrants to Victoria, the goal of becoming a gentleman farmer did not quickly fade. One of my great-grandfathers, Richard Ratcliffe Taylor, was an English immigrant who was a successful coal mine owner on the Prairies. In 1908, he retired to Victoria, building a large home at the corner of Lansdowne and Richmond Roads, across from what would become the Normal School (and eventually Camosun College). He named it Ormerod House, reputedly after an ancestral home in England. His gently sloping acreage, which included an orchard, gave beautiful views of the city and the Olympic Mountains. However, what might be called Untimely Death Syndrome (which afflicted Dunsmuir and Green) prevailed, for, after only three years in Victoria, he died in 1911. His coach house, made habitable, became the home of artist and singer Peggy Walton Packard, whose father purchased the Taylor home from Richard's widow. The residence itself was demolished and an apartment building constructed in its place.

3 *Colonist,* January 1, 1891, 4. The writer mistakenly identified the building material of Gyppeswyk as brick. (Note: While the Victoria *Daily Colonist* began life as the *British Colonist,* for the sake of brevity, I refer to it as simply *Colonist.*)

4 Mrs. W.J.H. Holmes (née Winnifred Worlock) to Flora Hamilton Burns, October 24, 1958 (BCA Vertical Files 56–0746).

5   Today, the paintings exhibited in the foyer, the Sara Spencer Gallery, and the Kearley Galleries show this love of manicured landscape. As well, two works by Sophie Pemberton show young people relaxing on the grass in or near orchards that could have been Gyppeswyk's.

6   At that time, the lot at Rockland and Moss was sold to James D. Ferguson, an insurance agent. By 1946, A.W. Millar owned this corner lot. In 1947, Herbert W. Davey purchased the remaining lot between the Ferguson/Millar property and Gyppeswyk. Mr. Davey, later a justice of the BC Supreme Court, was partner in the law firm of Crease, Davey, Lawson, Davis, Gordon and Baker—with its links to the Crease family living at Pentrelew on Fort Street.

7   The stone wall that stands on the north side of the property today was probably erected when Wilspencer Place was created. A similar wall may have stood on Moss Street as well but was removed because it was an impediment to the builders of the annexes added in the 1950s and 1970s. Along Pentrelew Place this structure becomes a retaining wall.

8   Martin Segger and Douglas Franklin, *Victoria: A Primer for Regional History in Architecture* (Watkins Glen, New York: American Life Foundation and Study Institute, 1979), 271. Among other Ridgway Wilson mansions were Newcombe House (138 Dallas Road; 1908), 1611 Quadra Street, and Patley (1617 Rockland Avenue; 1905). Robin Ward suggests that Elmer Wilson began the designs for Gyppeswyk but, upon ending his partnership with Wilson, turned over the work to the younger architect. (Robin Ward, *Echoes of Empire: Victoria and its Remarkable Buildings* [Madeira Park, BC: Harbour, 1996], 250.)

9   *Colonist*, June 15, 1889, 4.

10 *Colonist*, January 1, 1891, 7.

11 Although much of the mansion is still intact, some areas are not, so I use the past tense here. Where features of the house are extant, I indicate the fact by using the present tense.

12 Clarence Cook, "The House Beautiful," in *Late Victorian Decor from Eastlake's Gothic to Cook's House Beautiful*, ed. Hugh Guthrie (New York: American Life Foundation, 1968), 125–28.

13 Guthrie, *Late Victorian Decor*, passim. (Did any of the younger Green, Worlock, or Spencer boys ever try sliding down this banister?)

14 The interior, says Robin Ward, is "quirky," looking like "an eccentric club that meets for tea in the dining room" (Ward, *Echoes of Empire*, 250).

15 The first gas works in Victoria were established in 1859 near Rock Bay. Pipes were being laid in the city's main streets by 1862. The decor guru Clarence Cook preferred soft candlelight to harsh gas lighting. (Cook, in Guthrie, *Late Victorian Decor*, 160–62.) Gas fixtures were noisy; they sizzled, and could also damage furniture and fabrics. The brilliance of gas, however, satisfied the age's concern for brightness, which was equated with cleanliness. (Candles were messy.)

16 Cook, in Guthrie, *Late Victorian Decor*, 156.

17 Charles L. Eastlake, "Hints on Household Taste," in *Late Victorian Decor from Eastlake's Gothic to Cook's House Beautiful*, ed. Hugh Guthrie (New York: American Life Foundation, 1968), 179.

18 This situation would change in the later years of the Spencers' occupancy when the cook, Ho, occupied a suite of rooms on the second floor.

19 A bull's-eye window is round.

20 The headline read "Another Palatial Residence." (*Colonist*, May 28, 1889, 3.)

THE FOUNDING FAMILY

1 Although Alexander Green, who commissioned Gyppeswyk in 1889, came to Victoria after the arrival of the mansion's later owner, David Spencer, in 1863, I describe the Green family first, in order to set the scene, as it were, on the site of the house. Readers who are puzzled by this disynchronicity should consult the Time Line in Appendix II.

2 Derek Pethick calls 1858, when gold was discovered on the Fraser River, "the most fateful year in British Columbia's history" (Derek Pethick, *Men of British Columbia* [Victoria: Hancock, 1975], 79).

3 Henry Crease to Sarah Crease, April 12, 1859, quoted in Kathryn Bridge, *Henry & Self: The Private Life of Sarah Crease 1826–1922* (Victoria: Sono Nis, 1996), 68.

4 Matthew MacFie, *Vancouver Island and British Columbia: Their History, Resources and Prospects* (London: Longman, Green, Longman, Roberts & Grant, 1865), 79.

5 The standard of living was relatively high, with the Fort Victoria mess room tables set with linen tablecloths and crystal decanters, and flanked by Windsor chairs. (Michael Kluckner, *Victoria: The Way It Was* [North Vancouver: Whitecap, 1986], 12 and 15.)

6 Margaret Ormsby, *British Columbia: A History* (Toronto: Macmillan, 1958), 141.

7 Vivienne Chadwick, "The Green Family Grew with British Columbia," *Colonist*, April 24, 1966, 2.

8 Some sources maintain that Ferndale was built with prefabricated iron left over from the "Iron Church" donated by Baroness Burdett-Coutts in 1859. (Impractical due to the noise falling rain made on its metallic roof, the church was later demolished.)

9 By 1893, Ferndale was up for sale, with the purchaser required to remove the house, presumably because of the construction of the new Legislative Buildings. (*Colonist*, July 30, 1893, 1.)

10 Carr seems to have envied the relaxed, easy-going atmosphere of the Green household. ("The Book of Small," in *Complete Writings of Emily Carr* [Vancouver: Douglas & McIntyre, 1993], 186.)

11 So wrote the *Cowichan Leader* (n.d., 1967, BCA MS 2259, Box 10, File 14). Among the success stories associated with Gyppeswyk, similar destinies abound. The later owner of Green's house, David Spencer, also left Britain seeking gold in the new world, as did architect John Teague (1835–1902), Spencer's future brother-in-law. Thomas McInnes, the lieutenant-governor who lived at Gyppeswyk from 1899–1900, was a trained physician. Alexander Green and Colin Graham—both residents at Gyppeswyk for a short time—were sons of doctors and both studied medicine as young men.

12 *Colonist*, September 22, 1891, 5.

13 Ellis and Company, "Victoria Illustrated," *Colonist*, 1891, 62.

14 The directors of the orphanage invested in Alexander Green's bank and must have experienced some concern when it failed. (See, for example, *Colonist*, December 20, 1906, 6.)

15 *Colonist*, September 22, 1891, 5.

16 *Colonist*, September 25, 1891, 3.

17 His niece, Winnifred Worlock, remembered him as "one of the kindest men" she had ever known. (Quoted in a letter from Flora Hamilton Burns to James K. Nesbitt, November 19, 1958 [BCA Vertical Files 56-0746].) His wide circle of friends and acquaintances, as well as the respect with which he was held, is reflected in the fact that he was often listed as a pallbearer for local funerals.

18 *Colonist*, September 25, 1891, 3. At one point in his life, Chantrell (d. 1917) was an ordained minister, living on Kingston Street and working as an assistant to Bishop Cridge at the Church of Our Lord, where the Greens worshipped.

19 W. & J. Wilson Clothiers was founded in 1862. Terry Reksten (*More*

English than the English: A very social history of Victoria [Victoria: Orca, 1986], 159) wrote that W. and J. Wilson have been "at the corner of Government and Trounce Alley . . . on the same site since the 1860s," and, according to their website, W. & J. Wilson "have always conducted business from this location." These statements are not quite accurate, for the Wilsons' address was first 83 Government Street, whereas the Wells Fargo / Garesche Green business was at 81 Government, exactly the northeast corner of Government and Trounce Alley. (The 1885 Fire Insurance plan for Victoria, for example shows "Bank - Wells Fargo" at 83 Government and W. & J. Wilson next door to the north at 83.) By 1900, the Canadian Pacific Telegraph Office had moved into the bank/express offices at 81, and Wilson's Clothiers were still next-door. It was not until 1912 that the Wilson brothers expanded, taking over the premises at 81 Government, where the clothier business does indeed still operate today.

[20] Ellis, "Victoria Illustrated," 62. Their 1889 advertisement stated: "Deposits received in Gold, Silver and United States currency. Interest paid in the same on Time Deposits. Gold Dust and U.S. currency purchased at highest market rates. Sight Drafts and Telegraphic Transfers on San Francisco, New York and Canada. Exchange on London available in all parts of Europe, England, Ireland and Scotland. Letters of credit issued on the principal cities of the United States, Canada and Europe" (*Williams' Victoria Directory*, comp. Thomas Draper [Victoria: Williams, 1889], opp. p. 156).

[21] J.P. Elford and A.J. Smith were brickmakers and contractors based on Douglas Street near Topaz Avenue. (Elford came to Victoria from Australia.)

[22] *Colonist*, September 29, 1891, 7.

[23] Her relatively unusual name means "friend of God" in classical Greek.

[24] In the "A.A. Green Collection" at the BC Archives, an undated, unsigned typescript document in a Vertical File maintains that Green came first to Victoria, and then went back to England in 1873, where he married Theophila. However, this seems unlikely since UK vital statistics note that the couple married in 1872 and Theophila gave birth to their first children in 1873—in England.

[25] The 1891 Victoria census lists as living at Gyppeswyk one "Genn Bertha Green" (or Bertha Green Genn?), twenty-one years old, born in England, as governess. Was she a relative of Alexander Green? The UK

and Canadian vital statistics records have no record of any person with precisely this name. A "Bertha Genn" of Victoria was the co-respondent in a local divorce case, and proceeded to have a sensational life, but it seems unlikely that the Greens would have hired her as a governess.

26 In my experience, some English expatriates in Victoria maintained this attitude well into the 1960s.

27 *Colonist*, December 4, 1896, 5.

28 *Colonist*, August 26, 1930, 1; *Times*, August 26, 1930, 1. Ray Green is buried in the family plot.

29 *Colonist*, September 5, 1963, 7. Elsewhere, Nesbitt noted that Green's speeches "rambled" (*Colonist*, January 3, 1954, 31).

30 *Cowichan Leader*, 1967, clipping from BC Gazette List of Surveyors (BC Archives clipping file, MS 2259, Box 10, File 14).

31 *Colonist*, July 14, 1896, 8.

32 Chadwick, "The Green Family," *Colonist*, April 24, 1966, 2.

33 *The Book of Small*, 151. The names of these servants are not given in the 1891 census, perhaps because they were unintelligible to the census takers or because the Greens, answering for their servants, did not attach personal identities to their Asian employees.

34 Chadwick, "The Green Family," 2.

JUST VISITING

1 *Colonist*, May 21, 1893, 7.

2 Mrs. William Holmes (née Winnifred Worlock) to Flora Hamilton Burns, October 24, 1858 (BCA Vertical Files, 56-0746). However, Winnifred Worlock remembered both families living there until 1899, a ménage that would not have included Frank William Green, who was at medical school in Montreal. Moreover, city directories indicate that between 1895 and 1899 Frederick Worlock and his son Montague (Ray) lived on Rockland Avenue, Vancouver Street, and finally Pemberton Road. Did Frederick and Ray move out, leaving Gyppeswyk to Theophila and Martha and the younger children? Perhaps even the Green Mansion was too small to accommodate three adults and at least eight young people. Winnifred may have remembered only a period of two years before all the Worlocks moved out, a period which could have been either great fun or deeply annoying to young people. Or possibly she recalled a largely feminine household, which endured until 1899.

[3] *Times*, July 31, 1926, 2.

[4] *Colonist*, February 14, 1893, 9.

[5] *Vancouver Province*, August 2, 1926 (Vertical File, BCA).

[6] *Colonist*, March 3, 1894, 5.

[7] *Colonist*, December 11, 1895, 6; March 3, 1894, 5.

[8] *Times*, April 13, 1894, 4.

[9] *Province*, August 2, 1926 (Vertical File, BCA).

[10] James Marsh, ed. *The Canadian Encyclopedia* (Edmonton: Hurtig, 1988), 1: 172.

[11] *Province*, August 2, 1926 (Vertical File, BCA).

[12] The "Lancers" was a dance similar to the quadrille, in which four couples assumed a square formation, an early form of modern square dancing. (*Colonist*, November 2, 1893, 5.)

THE LIEUTENANT-GOVERNORS

[1] *Colonist*, quoting an edition from 1897, February 18, 1951, 11.

[2] *Colonist*, 19 May 1899, 2. James K. Nesbitt cheekily described the "plump" lieutenant-governor escaping the flames, puffing his frantic way along a smoky corridor at Cary Castle. ("Old Homes and Families," *Colonist Magazine*, February 18, 1951, 11.)

[3] N. de Bertrand Lugrin, "McInnes Last In Office at Old Cary Castle," *Times Sunday Magazine*, August 16, 1952, 5. It is nearly a tradition for the Queen's vice-regal representatives in BC to accommodate a temporary move from the official residence. The "custom" began when Governor Arthur Kennedy had to reside in the Joseph Trutch home (Fairfield House) in 1864 while renovations were made to Cary Castle. As we have seen, the Worlock Cottage on Rockland Avenue served a similar function. In 1957, when Government House burned yet again, the Empress Hotel was the vice-regent's temporary home. A further example of the close ties between Victorians at this time is the fact that David Spencer's department store supplied the architect Samuel Maclure with the furnishings needed for the reconstruction of Government House, which was completed in 1903, the year that Spencer purchased Gyppeswyk.

[4] I have not been able to ascertain who tended the grounds at Gyppeswyk at this time or earlier. The lieutenant-governor may have brought his own domestic staff with him to the mansion, but some of the gardeners at

Cary Castle probably stayed on there to maintain the property during reconstruction. As well, we don't know if the Greens' Chinese servants remained at Gyppeswyk after 1899.

5   "Hardly a seemly affair," he adds (S.W. Jackman, *The Men of Cary Castle: A Series of Portrait Sketches of the Lieutenant-Governors of British Columbia from 1871–1971* [Victoria: Morriss, 1972], 75).

6   Jackman, *Men of Cary Castle*, 70.

7   Quoted in James K. Nesbitt, "Old Homes and Families," *Colonist Magazine*, February 18, 1951, 11.

8   John Tupper Saywell, quoted in *Colonist*, March 8, 1959, 4.

9   James Nesbitt, "His Honor Forgiven," *Colonist*, February 8, 1957, 4.

10   *Colonist*, May 27, 1906, 4.

11   Unpublished manuscript, March 4, 1933 (Vertical Files D–19 0 55 BCA).

12   *Times*, January 2, 1901, 3.

13   *Colonist*, October 2, 1901, 3.

14   *Times*, October 2, 1901, 2. Some of the pageantry and verbiage occasioned by the royal visit may seem quaint or overblown today. In the "Royal Souvenir Edition" of the *Daily Times* (October 1901, 4), for instance, the second verse of a local poet's tribute—"Imperium et Libertas. Ode to the Duke and Duchess of Cornwall"—included these nearly incomprehensible lines:

> Welcome, oh thou, rich in pious strain
> Of fair descent! Hail to thy gracious spouse!
> May not the less the virtue that endows
> Thy sovereign mother duly grace the reign
> Of thy dear Princess!

15   Interview with Sylvia Graham, June 30, 2011.

DAVID SPENCER AND HIS BUSINESS

1   *Colonist*, June 30, 1917, 10.

2   The source for this episode in young David Spencer's life is a booklet published by the *Colonist* on the occasion of the store's golden jubilee in 1923. (*David Spencer Ltd. Golden Jubilee 1873–1923* [Victoria: Colonist Press, 1923], 3.)

3   Peter Johnson, *Voyages of Hope: the Saga of the Bride-Ships* (Victoria: TouchWood Editions, 2002), 196. At least one other historian, Derek Pethick (see *Summer of Promise: Victoria 1864–1914* [Victoria: Sono Nis, 1980], 87), as well as journalists writing in the the Victoria *Daily Times*

and Victoria *Daily Colonist* have assumed that Spencer did spend time in the Cariboo.

4 Patrick Dunae, *Gentlemen Emigrants: From the British Public Schools to the Canadian Frontier* (Vancouver: Douglas & McIntyre, 1981), 39.

5 The possibility that Spencer had panned for gold there has been buttressed by the fact that on July 15, 1867, the *Cariboo Sentinel* in Barkerville carried a small notice about his wedding to Emma. Because a Wesleyan Methodist church functioned in Barkerville, Spencer might have had acquaintances there, or perhaps the editor merely copied the notice from a Victoria newspaper. In any case, no record of his own residence in Barkerville seems to have survived.

6 In Victoria at this time, wrote the British journalist Matthew Macfie, "small retailers and mechanics swarm among the Methodists ... The bankers, lawyers and wholesale dealers prefer the Church of England" (*Vancouver Island and British Columbia: Their History, Resources and Prospects* [London: Longman, Green, Longman, Roberts & Grant, 1865], 417). Macfie was correct because Spencer was still a "small" retailer—the Anglican Alexander Green, was, of course, a banker.

7 May 6, 1906, 3.

8 His political views are not easy to discover, but *c.* 1870 his store was an agent for the newspaper of democrat Amor de Cosmos, *The Daily Standard.* (Of course, he may have sold other newspapers as well.)

9 Temperance advocates supported the abolition of the manufacture and sale of alcoholic beverages—a not unwise position at a time when alcoholism was rampant and ruining families but still without effective treatment. Spencer's support of the Temperance movement may have been challenged by the social activities of the Arion Male Voice Choir, of which he was member. "The early social events of the Arion Club,'" writes the club's historian, "were extremely 'wet,'" with much "eating, smoking and drinking involved" (R. Dale McIntosh, *One Hundred Years of Singing: the Arion Male Voice Choir of Victoria, BC, Canada* [Victoria: Beach Holme, 1992], 7 and 49).

10 This could have been the "Frederick Street" in Victoria West between Russell Street and the Songhees Reservation (now Dundas Street) or the Frederick Street running east of Quadra Street (now Balmoral Road).

11 *Times*, March 2, 1920, 4.

12 MacFie, *Vancouver Island and British Columbia*, 396.

13 Significantly, the Spencers are not mentioned in Valerie Green's account of Victoria's aristocracy, *Above Stairs: Social Life in Upper-Class Victoria 1843–1918* (Victoria: Sono Nis, 1995). Nor do they seem to have been active members of the Union Club (Paul L. Bissley, *Early and Later Victorians: A History of the Union Club of BC* [Sidney: Review, 1969]). Although prominent in business life in Victoria and Vancouver, Spencer is not caricatured in a volume of images published by the Newspaper Cartoonists Association of BC (*British Columbians as We See 'Em: 1910 and 1911* [Vancouver: News Advertiser, *c.* 1911]).

14 *Colonist*, September 9, 1903.

15 The *Times* devoted a long, laudatory editorial to Spencer on March 4, 1920 (4).

16 Jamie Morton, "David Spencer," in *Dictionary of Canadian Biography: 1911–1920* (Volume XIV).

17 *Colonist*, March 3, 1920, 1. Researcher Chris Hanna notes that the Wilson brothers found him ill-mannered, self-absorbed, and mercenary. (Correspondence, December 1, 2011.)

18 Elmer H. Fisher (1840–1905) was an American architect who also designed several buildings in Vancouver, Port Townsend, and Seattle.

19 Thomas Hooper (1887–1935) was born in England, came to Canada in 1891, and made his way to Victoria in 1889. He designed the new Metropolitan Methodist Church on Pandora Avenue—the Spencers' church—as well as the Gorge Road Methodist Church. The contractors for the Five Sisters Block were the prolific and enduring Luney Brothers.

20 *Colonist*, April 5, 1896, 7.

21 *Times*, June 29, 1917, 9.

22 *Colonist*, December 13, 1908, 16. By 1933, the Victoria store employed four hundred and thirty-five full-time people. (*Colonist*, October 1, 1933, 8.) See also *Colonist*, December 1, 1948, 18.

23 An advertisement in Ellis, "Victoria Illustrated," *The Daily Colonist*, 1891, 86.

24 Ellis, "Victoria Illustrated," 86.

25 *Colonist*, December 13, 1908, 16; *Times*, June 29, 1917, 9.

26 *Colonist*, December 13, 1908, 16.

27 *Colonist*, June 30, 1917, 10.

28 The career of Timothy Eaton (1834–1907) parallels that of David Spencer and his sons. He, too, was born on the periphery of the British Isles, in Ulster, and trained as an apprentice shopkeeper. Having immigrated to

Canada, he opened a dry goods store in St. Mary's, Ontario, and purchased another in Toronto in 1869. If it had been David Spencer who first discovered the efficacy of the mail-order catalogue, and not Timothy Eaton, one chapter of Canadian business history would be written differently. In any event, Eaton's enterprise lasted much longer. Ironically, the Hudson's Bay Company eventually took over the Victoria Eaton's store, which now stands on the site of Spencer's business. The HBC founded Victoria and remains at the heart of the twenty-first-century city. (But for how long?)

EMMA SPENCER AND HER CHILDREN

[1] Ainslie J. Helmcken, "View Street ended Abruptly," *Colonist Islander*, May 7, 1967, 11.

[2] James K. Nesbitt, "Old Homes and Families," *Colonist*, February 1, 1948, 7.

[3] *Times*, June 29, 1917, 9.

[4] *Colonist*, May 10, 1924, 5.

[5] Fawcett, *Some Reminiscences of Old Victoria*, 290.

[6] John Nelson, "Romance of the House of Spencer," *Maclean's*, vol. 38, no.17 (September 1, 1925), 26.

[7] Nelson, "Romance," 26.

[8] *Times*, June 30, 1917, 17.

[9] *Western Methodist Recorder*, 1922 (BCA Vertical Files, 56ff.).

[10] *Times*, October 1, 1923.

[11] *Colonist*, May 10, 1924, 5.

[12] In 1900, the average age at first marriage for males was 25.9 years; for females, it was 21.9 years. One can only speculate as to why these Spencer children stayed single for so long.

[13] *Colonist*, December 13, 1908, 16.

[14] James K. Nesbitt, "David Spencer's Family: A British Columbia Saga," *Colonist*, December 1, 1948, 7; *Colonist*, June 22, 1932, 2. Others have described him "austere" (his brother-in-law Gerald McGeer) and "mercenary" (David Ricardo Williams, *Mayor Gerry: The Remarkable Gerald Grattan McGeer* [Vancouver: Douglas & McIntyre, 1986], 33 and 121).

[15] Nesbitt, "David Spencer's Family," and *Colonist*, May 17, 1898, 5.

[16] *Colonist*, November 30, 1897, 5; *Colonist*, May 17, 1898, 5.

[17] Nesbitt, "David Spencer's Family." Later in life, diverging from his father's ways, he became a "heavy-drinking man" (Williams, *Mayor Gerry*, 121).

18 Nesbitt, "Family."

19 Nesbitt, "Family."

20 Audrey Johnson, "Carr Fuelled Drive for Art Gallery," *Times Colonist Islander*, July 16, 1989, C7.

21 *Times*, June 29, 1917, 9.

22 *Colonist*, September 14, 1958, 19. "She was a grand girl," said Colin Graham, "extremely able and extremely modest," "flustered by . . . praise." Commenting on her "aversion to the limelight," her niece Myfanwy Pavelic described her as a "rare person," "a gentlewoman with every breath she took" (*Times Colonist*, January 9, 1983, A3).

23 Mrs. Graham found Ho to be "well-spoken" (Interview, 11 November 2010). The name "Ho" is not uncommon among the Chinese of Victoria but perhaps this man was the one described in the census of 1901 as a twenty-year-old "cook." (No address is given but possibly he was the man cooking meals at Gyppeswyk in the 1940s.) One of the attic rooms is still lined with wallpaper in a chinoiserie pattern, which could have been a nod in the direction of the ethnic background of the servant who lived there, or simply an unintended, ironic compliance with what was in vogue at the time.

24 Interview with Sylvia Graham, November 11, 2010.

25 Williams, *Mayor Gerry*, 30.

A SHOWPLACE MANSION

1 Carr in 1934 in a letter to Eric Brown, director of the National Gallery of Canada, quoted in Doris Shadbolt, *Preface to Emily Carr*, Vancouver Art Gallery catalogue, 1971, 5.

2 *Times*, October 13, 1951, 11.

3 In 1956, in the spirit of Josephine Crease and Sara Spencer, Alan Douglas Ford, a local millionaire, offered to bequeath his Terrace Avenue home, Tancred—a Tudor Revival house built by James Kilvington Worsfold in 1904—to the Art Gallery of Greater Victoria. The bequest would have included the contents of the house as well as its garden, "fully endowed," presumably to be used as a satellite gallery and/or a fundraising tourist attraction. At the time, the board of directors advised Colin Graham to accept the bequest, but only on certain terms. (Minutes, October 24, 1956 [AGGV].) Tact and discretion, if not actual secrecy, surrounded the proceedings, for the paper trail is thin. All that seems to have survived

is an un-dated onionskin copy of a letter from Graham to "Dear Mr. F. . . ." (name omitted), in which he notes that the arts centre did not have enough staff even to maintain its Moss Street space, and so recommended that "Mr. F." increase the endowment to allow for the hiring of someone to administer the house (AGGV). Obviously, Tancred did not become a part of the Art Gallery of Greater Victoria but, upon his death in 1967, Ford made a generous donation to the gallery.

4   Board of Directors' Minutes, AGGV, June 16, 1951. Technically, Sara offered the mansion on behalf of the Spencer Foundation.

5   *Times*, June 29, 1917, 9.

6   John Adams, *The Ker Family of Victoria 1859–1976* (Vancouver: Holte, 2007), 254.

7   *Colonist*, July 18, 1951, 1. Victoria's ambivalent attitude toward the visual arts is perhaps illustrated by the *Colonist*'s page one headline for the Ireland interview. The archivist had approved of the City taking over the Spencer Mansion, but the headline read, "House Held Unsuitable for Priceless Paintings," which contradicted the gist of Ireland's views.

8   How one volunteer, Gwladys Downes, described what followed the initial gift. (AGGV, "Art Gallery History" file, January 1995.)

9   *Times*, June 18, 1977, 34.

10 See Colin Graham, *Moss Street Years; or Three Decades of Controversial Hangings*, unpublished manuscript, 1981, 19–20.

11 Colin Graham to Myfanwy Pavelic (Director's Correspondence File, November 14, 1955, AGGV). To the members of the board, the curator/director expressed what many in the community believed, that the City Council's attitude toward the arts centre was not only "dilatory" but "either grossly insulting or grossly incompetent" (*Arts Centre Bulletin*, September 1954, AGGV). Fortunately, matters have improved greatly over the last half-century.

12 G.N. Stacey (secretary of Spencer Realties Ltd.) to J. Ronald Grant (president, arts centre board of directors), October 15, 1952, AGGV.

13 Audrey St. Denys Johnson, "Art Centre has it First Display," Victoria *Daily Times*, November 21, 1951, 16.

14 Mayor Harrison had doubts about the wisdom of his attending the ceremony. In a letter to "J. Roland [sic] Grant," he reminded the arts centre president that, as yet, there had been "no legal transfer of any kind from the owners of 1040 Moss Street" and that therefore the opening "maybe

[sic] somewhat premature." "I do not agree that the time is ripe for such an opening as arrangements have not been completed." In order not to "cause embarrassment to His Excellency," however, he agreed to attend (September 29, 1952, AGGV).

15 Unpublished page proofs for Audrey St. Denys Johnson's *Arts Beat*, Chapter 22, page 257 (AGGV).

16 With an MD from Queen's University, he came to Vancouver in 1909 and set up practice. In 1943, he moved to live and work in Victoria. He died in 1946. Graham's maternal grandfather was also a medical doctor.

17 "Colin Graham," *Arts Victoria*, November 1978, Vol. IV, no. 3, 7.

18 "City needs Art Watchdog to Ban Banal Architecture. Landscape Blighted by Unending Sameness," *Colonist*, December 15, 1960, 5.

19 June 22, 1951; July 19, 1951 (AGGV). How these ladies could have been so mistaken is possibly due to their having been given only a cursory tour of the mansion and perhaps, while on that tour, not seriously considering any part of it as comfortable living quarters. Actually, the Grahams would have preferred a detached house with "a garden of our own, preferably near some open country" (Letter to Mrs. Uhthoff, July 13, 1951 AGGV). Probably aware of this wish, Mrs. Wyllie told Graham about a "nice little garden with vegetables at the back [of the mansion] which I am sure anyone staying in the house could use" (July 19, 1951). Perhaps this amenity convinced them to accept the prospect of a "nice" suite.

20 Interview with Sylvia Graham, November 11, 2010.

21 Board of Directors' Minutes, January 8, 1952 and April 2, 1952 (AGGV).

22 Interview with Sylvia Graham, November 11, 2010.

23 The Grahams had three sons: Alan, who lived as a baby for a few months at Gyppeswyk between 1952 and 1953, trained as an architect, and is now retired; James, a professor of New Media at Lethbridge University; and John, an active Vancouver architect, who designed the Grahams' retirement home at Deep Cove.

24 *Times*, May 4, 1957, 6.

25 Gwladys Downes, "Some Notes on the History of the Art Gallery of Greater Victoria," February 24, 1994 (AGGV).

26 Notable was the "Intimate Stage," an amateur shoestring summer company of mainly university students under the direction of first Flora Nicholson in the 1950s, and later Tony Nicholson, which produced avant-garde and rarely seen (at least not in Victoria) plays by John Osborne,

August Strindberg, and Eugene Ionesco, in the drawing room and on—literally—the grand staircase in 1959 and 1960.

[27] Downes, "Some Notes." Ironically, at least one of these supper-dances (in December 1958) had an East Asian theme, with Chinese food served by Chinese waiters in an atmosphere lit by Chinese lanterns. "Times had changed but we may wonder if the Greens and Worlocks would have been surprised or even approved . . ."

[28] *Times*, October 15, 1952, 1.

[29] *Colonist*, October 14, 1951, 5. He was being diplomatic. In his later reminiscences, he wrote that the house "offered a less than ideal solution to the problems of creating a permanent civic gallery" (*The Moss Street Years*, 16).

[30] *Colonist*, July 28, 1951, 1.

[31] *Times*, February 8, 1952, 13.

[32] Gwen Cash, "Seven Year Art Battle," February 22, 1952, unattributed newspaper article (AGGV scrapbook). Since the 1970s, the three main-floor rooms are no longer used for exhibitions, due to insurance limitations. Instead, they now display nineteenth- and early-twentieth-century paintings from the permanent collection that are appropriate to the historic decor.

DISCREET ALTERATIONS

[1] In September 1958, the centre's monthly bulletin noted that "discreet alterations" were still being made to the mansion (*Art Centre Bulletin*, 1958, AGGV).

[2] Minutes of the Board of Directors meeting, March 19, 1957 (AGGV).

[3] Minutes of the Board of Directors meetings, November 18 and December 11, 1956 (AGGV).

[4] Minutes of the Board of Directors meeting, September 9, 1969 (AGGV).

[5] Minutes of the Board of Directors meetings, March 12, April 16, and October 30, 1974 (AGGV).

[6] Roger Boulet, "Plan for Development" (AGGV).

[7] "City" File Correspondence, 1951–53 (AGGV).

[8] *Times*, August 9, 1952 (AGGV scrapbook).

[9] J. Ronald Grant, to mayor and council, September 17, 1952 (AGGV).

[10] Minutes of the Board of Directors meeting, October 8, 1963 (AGGV).

[11] Assessors' Report, in "Requirements for a Fireproof Wing" (AGGV). The

original assessors were Brahm Wiesman, director of the regional planning board, Ross A. Lort, a Vancouver architect, and Colin Graham. Lort was replaced by Wilfred Ussner, of the University of British Columbia architecture department.

12 Constructing only one of the proposed additions would, of course, have been less expensive. In any event, the competition produced several interesting plans, at least one of which was very costly. One proposal dutifully involved using the north facade for a sole addition, leaving the porte-cochère intact. Another envisaged a larger, two-part addition with one wing on the north side and another at the front (east side), which would have necessitated the removal of the porte-cochère. Another massive proposal suggested demolishing Gyppeswyk completely and constructing a new, large, dramatically designed art gallery. This two-storey structure would have covered the entire property and included an auditorium.

13 *Arts Centre Bulletin*, January–February 1958 (AGGV). In 1951, after the mansion had been turned over to the arts centre, forty unhealthy trees had to be cut down; others were pruned. (Interview with Sylvia Graham, November 11, 2010.)

14 In January 1960, another addition, the glass-fronted Ker Memorial Gallery, was opened. This was a long, narrow room on the east side of the south Centennial Gallery, designed by James Polson and Robert Siddall. Other additions were made to the modern wings, the Founders and Drury Galleries in 1970, and the Pollard Wing in 1977. These rooms greatly enlarged the space of the whole modern addition and included ramps for people in wheelchairs.

15 Minutes of the Board of Directors meeting, October 15, 1957 (AGGV); Emery to Clack, February 17, 1959 (AGGV). The new structure was funded by the province through a BC Centennial Grant and by the municipalities of Victoria, Saanich, Esquimalt, and Oak Bay. A generous donation from local businessman Robert Ker, and a Canada Council grant, also helped considerably.

16 Letter to Colin Graham, February 21, 1959 (AGGV).

17 Reksten, *More English than the English*, 163.

18 Victoria Heritage Foundation, *This Old House: Victoria's Heritage Neighbourhoods. Volume Three: Rockland, Burnside, Harris Green, Hillside-Quadra, North Park, Oaklands* (Victoria: Printorium, 2007), 145.

19 Ward, *Echoes of Empire*, 1996, 249.

[20] "Hundreds and Thousands," in *Complete Writings*, 776.

[21] Minutes of the annual meeting of the Women's Committee, 1958 (AGGV). Nevertheless, the germ of the modern architectural heritage movement can be seen in the brief sent to the provincial cabinet from the Victoria branch of the BC Historical Association in 1957. With the burning of the last "Birdcage," this group began to fear that "our links with the past are going." However, they made no mention of the plans for Gyppeswyk. (*Colonist*, June 15, 1957, 15.) A co-author of the brief to the cabinet was Robert Ker, who was helping to fund the new wing.

[22] April 26, 1956, "A.G.M." (AGGV). He makes no mention of this matter in his memoirs, *Moss Street Years*.

[23] Letter to Flora Hamilton Burns, November 10, 1958. (BCA Clippings, Vertical File 56-0746.) A later director, Roget Boulet, suggested that Gyppeswyk be granted heritage designation. In 1980, another director, Patricia Bovey, inquired into the application procedure for according Gyppeswyk heritage protection. The terms of the Heritage Conservation Act of British Columbia, however, require that major features of a building be intact. The removal of the porte-cochère as well as the transformation of several of the main-floor rooms, including the library, prevents such a designation.

[24] Graham, *Moss Street Years*, 81. The chronology here may be faulty, because Sylvia Graham remembers "a young couple named Rhodes" moving into the upstairs suite when she and Colin vacated it in early 1953, whereas Colin, in his memoirs, writes that the Davises moved in at that time. The board minutes agree with Colin but the city directory has the Rhodes (and not the Davises) in residence in 1954. Conceivably, memory has proved unreliable or the board's secretary has confused names.

[25] June 22, 1955, AGGV (personnel file).

[26] *Arts Victoria*, Vol. III, no. 2, April 1977, 14.

[27] Interview with Sylvia Graham, November 11, 2010.

[28] Minutes of the Board of Directors meeting, May 8, 1962 (AGGV).

[29] Minutes of the Board of Directors meeting, May 12, 1964 (AGGV).

[30] Minutes of the Board of Directors meeting, October 7, 1952 (AGGV).

[31] October 10, 1955, AGGV (personnel file); Minutes of the Board of Directors meeting, September 12, 1956 (AGGV).

[32] Minutes of the annual meeting of the Women's Committee, 1959 (AGGV).

[33] *Bulletin of the Art Gallery of Greater Victoria*, November–December 1968, 3.

[34] Minutes of the Board of Directors meetings, October 11, 1966 and December 13, 1966. In April 1967, the board was still mulling over the state of this basement room, wondering if furniture should be provided "to make the suite more suitable" (Minutes of the Board of Directors meeting, April 11, 1967, AGGV).

[35] Graham, *Moss Street Years*, 34.

INTO THE 21ST CENTURY

[1] Minutes of the Board of Directors meeting, March 12, 1968 (AGGV).

[2] Mr. Stark's words (Letter, April 26, 2011). Stuart Stark is a Victoria native, born in 1952. He has degrees from the University of Victoria and the University of British Columbia.

BIBLIOGRAPHY

PRIMARY SOURCES

Annual Reports for the Corporation of the City of Victoria.

Arts Victoria.

Bulletin of the Arts Centre of Greater Victoria.

Minutes of the Meetings of the Board of Directors, Art Gallery of Greater Victoria.

Minutes of the Meetings of the Women's Committee, Art Gallery of Greater Victoria.

Vancouver and Victoria City Directories.

BOOKS

Adams, John. *The Ker Family of Victoria* 1859–1976. Vancouver: Holte, 2007.

Adams, John. *Old Square-Toes and His Lady: The Life of James and Amelia Douglas.* Victoria: Horsdal & Schubart, 2001. ·

Bissley, Paul. L. *Early and Late Victorians. A History of the Union Club of BC.* Sidney: Review, 1969.

Blanchard, Paula. *The Life of Emily Carr.* Vancouver: Douglas & McIntyre, 1987.

Boam, Henry. *British Columbia: Its History, People, Commerce, Industries and Resources.* London: Sells, 1912.

Bridge, Kathryn. *Henry & Self: The Private Life of Sarah Crease 1826–1922.* Victoria: Sono Nis, 1996.

British Columbia Pictorial and Biographical. 2 vols. Vancouver: Clarke, 1914.

Carr, Emily. *The Complete Writings of Emily Carr.* Vancouver: Douglas & McIntyre, 1993.

Castle, Geoffrey. *[More] Victoria Landmarks. Victoria: [Castle and King].* Victoria: Sono Nis, 1985 and 1988.

Chamberlain, Paul G. *Victoria's Castles.* Victoria: Dingle House, 2005.

Cook, Clarence. "The Home Beautiful. New York 1877." In *Late Victorian Decor from Eastlake's Gothic to Cook's House Beautiful,* edited by Hugh Guthrie, 119–200. New York: American Life Foundation, 1968.

Corley-Smith, Peter. *Victoria Golf Club*. Victoria: Victoria Golf Club, 1992.

Cross, Rosemary. "William Ridgway Wilson." In *Building the West: The Early Architects of British Columbia*, edited by Donald Luxton. Vancouver: Talon, 2003.

"David Spencer." In *Encyclopedia of British Columbia*, 671. Madeira Park, BC: Harbour, 2000.

Eastlake, Charles L. "Hints on Household Taste. London, 1868." In *Late Victorian Decor from Eastlake's Gothic to Cook's House Beautiful*, edited by Hugh Guthrie, 7–116. New York: American Life Foundation, 1968.

Ellis and Company. "Victoria Illustrated." *The Daily Colonist*, 1891.

Ewert, Henry. *Victoria's Streetcar Era*. Victoria: Sono Nis, 1992.

Fawcett, Edgar. *Some Reminiscences of Old Victoria*. Toronto: Briggs, 1912.

Green, Valerie. *Above Stairs: Social Life in Upper-Class Victoria 1843–1918*. Victoria: Sono Nis, 1995.

Green, Valerie. *No Ordinary People: Victoria's Mayors since 1862*. Victoria: Beach Holme, 1992.

Hughes, Mary Jo, Michael Morris, and Barry Till. *Vision Into Reality: Art Gallery of Greater Victoria Early Years, 1951–1973*. Altona, Man.: Friesens, 2009.

Humphreys, Danda. *On the Street Where You Live*. 3 vols. Victoria: Heritage House, 1999–2001.

Jackman, S.W. *The Men of Cary Castle: A Series of Portrait Sketches of the Lieutenant-Governors of British Columbia from 1871–1971*. Victoria: Morriss, 1972.

Johnson, Audrey. *Arts Beat: The Arts in Victoria*. Victoria: Shillingford, 1994.

Johnson, Peter. *Voyages of Hope: the Saga of the Bride-Ships*. Victoria: TouchWood Editions, 2002.

Kerr, J.B. *Biographical Dictionary of Well-Known British Columbians*. BC: Kerr and Beg, 1890.

Kluckner, Michael. *Vancouver: The Way It Was*. Vancouver: Whitecap, 1984.

Kluckner, Michael. *Victoria: The Way it Was*. North Vancouver: Whitecap, c. 1986.

MacFie, Matthew. *Vancouver Island and British Columbia: Their History, Resources and Prospects*. London: Longman, Green, Longman, Roberts & Grant, 1865.

McGregor, D.A. *They Gave Royal Assent: The Lieutenant-Governors of British Columbia*. Vancouver: Mitchell, 1967.

McIntosh, Robert Dale. *One Hundred Years of Singing: the Arion Male Voice Choir of Victoria, BC, Canada*. Victoria: Beach Holme, 1992.

Morton, Jamie. "David Spencer." Vol. XIV, *Dictionary of Canadian Biography 1911–1920*. Toronto: University of Toronto, 2000.

Nesbitt, James Knight. *Album of Victoria Homes and Families*. Victoria: Hebden, 1956.

Ormsby, Margaret. *British Columbia: A History*. Toronto: Macmillan, 1958.

Pethick, Derek. *Men of British Columbia*. Victoria: Hancock, 1975.

Reksten, Terry. *Craigdarroch: The Story of Dunsmuir Castle*. Victoria: Orca, 1987.

Reksten, Terry. *More English than the English: A very social history of Victoria*. Victoria: Orca, 1986.

Segger, Martin and Douglas Franklin. *Exploring Victoria's Architecture*. Victoria: Sono Nis, 1996.

Segger, Martin. *A Primer for Regional History in Architecture*. Watkins Glen, New York: American Life Foundation and Study Institute, 1979.

Victoria Heritage Foundation. *This Old House: Victoria's Heritage Neighbourhoods. Volume Two: James Bay*. Victoria: Printorium, 2005.

—————*Volume Three: Rockland, Burnside, Harris Green, Hillside-Quadra, North Park, Oaklands*. Victoria: Printorium, 2007.

Ward, Robin. *Echoes of Empire: Victoria and its Remarkable Buildings*. Madeira Park: Harbour, 1996.

ELECTRONIC SOURCES

The British Colonist, 1858–1910 [www.britishcolonist.ca]

Census of Canada, 1881–1911 [www.collectionscanada.gc.ca]

Marriage and Death Records, British Columbia Archives [www.bcarchives. gov.bc.ca/index.htm]

Taylor, Leona and Dorothy Mindenhall, "Index of Historical Victoria Newspapers," *Victoria's Victoria*, 2007 [www.victoriasvictoria.ca]

United Kingdom Censuses [www.UKcensusOnline.com]

"Welsh Immigrant Who Built a Department Store Chain," *The Celtic Connection*, 2006 [www.celtic-connection.com/2006/features/ feat2006_05_03_hist.html]

PERIODICALS

Adams, John. "The Spencer Mansion at the Art Gallery of Greater Victoria." *Victoria Homes and Living Magazine* (Fall 2010): 20–24.

"Art Centre has its First Display." Victoria *Daily Times* (November 21, 1951): 16.

Chadwick, Vivienne. "The Green Family Grew with British Columbia." Victoria *Daily Colonist* (April 24, 1966): 2.

"D. Spencer, Ltd., Celebrates Golden Jubilee . . ." Victoria *Daily Times* (September 29, 1923): 14 and 22.

"Growth of a Great Mercantile House: David Spencer Limited." Victoria *Daily Colonist* (December 13, 1908): 16.

Johnson, Audrey. "Carr Fuelled Drive for Art Gallery." *Times Colonist Islander* (July 16, 1989): C7.

Johnson, Audrey. "Gallery is Graham's Best Work." *Times Colonist Islander* (September 17, 1990).

Litwin, Grania. "Painters Get Original at Victoria's Art Gallery." *Times Colonist* (July 15, 2004).

"Mr. and Mrs. David Spencer Will Celebrate The Fiftieth Anniversary of Their Wedding Tomorrow." Victoria *Daily Times* (June 29, 1917): 9.

Nelson, John. "Romance of the House of Spencer." *Maclean's*, vol. 38, no.17 (September 1, 1925): 26, 70–71.

Nesbitt, James K. "David Spencer's Family—a British Columbia Saga." Victoria *Daily Colonist* (December 1, 1948): 7.

"Pioneer Victorians Wedded 50 Years Ago." Victoria *Daily Colonist* (June 30, 1917): 10.

Wills, Archie. "Million Dollar Fire Ended View Street Blockade." Victoria *Daily Colonist* magazine (May 17, 1971): 6–7.

MISCELLANEOUS

Art Gallery of Greater Victoria. *Plans for the Art Gallery of Greater Victoria. An Invitation to Victorians to Participate in the Development of Their Gallery.* Victoria, 1962.

BC Artists' Tribute to Colin Graham (Victoria: Art Gallery of Greater Victoria, 1974). [exhibition]

Golden Jubilee. 1873–1923. David Spencer Ltd. Victoria: Colonist Press, 1923.

Graham, Colin D., "Moss Street Years: or Three Decades of Controversial Hangings" (unpublished manuscript, 1981).

Johnson, Audrey, "Arts Beat. The Arts in Victoria" (unpublished page proofs, *c.* 1994).

The Kearley Gallery: Self-Guided Tour (Victoria: Art Gallery of Greater Victoria). [pamphlet]

'Tis the Season with the Spencers. An Introduction to the Spencer Mansion (Victoria: Art Gallery of Greater Victoria, 2009). [pamphlet]

Victoria, BC. 1889 (Ellis and Co., 1889). [bird's-eye view]

Walden, F.W., "Social History of Victoria 1858–1871" (University of British Columbia MA Thesis, 1951).

INDEX

Spencer Mansion, additions, 4, 17–18, 128, 142, 150, 153–55; animals kept by residents, 14, 50; appearance, interior, 27–37, 128, 133, 145, 147, 149, 163–65; appearance, exterior, ii, 15, 17, 128, 156, 165; architectural styles, 14, 17, 18; architect: *see* Ridgway Wilson, William; Art Gallery of Greater Victoria, conversion to, 144, 149–52 (*see also* Art Gallery of Greater Victoria); belvedere, 9, 17, 18, 36, 165; conservatory, 17, 18, 32, 120, 128, 149 (*see also* Art Gallery of Greater Victoria: tea room); construction (1889), 11–12, 26, 37; dining room, 15, 21, 29, 32–33, 90, 128, 133, 147–50, 163–64 (*see also* Art Gallery of Greater Victoria: Kearley Gallery); donation to City of Victoria, 133–37; drawing room, 26–27, 31, 33, 35, 133, 147, 151, 163–64 (*see also* Art Gallery of Greater Victoria: Spencer Gallery); fireplaces, 18, 23, 26, 28–29, 31–32, 35–36, 149, 151, 164–65 (*see also* tiles); fire hazards, 141, 144, 145; fireproofing, 155, 165; flooring, 33, 35, 148–49; floor plans, (*c.* 1951 and 2012) 16; (*c.* 1977) 146, 148; gardens, 14, 33, 37, 66, 127, 151–53, 159, 164; Green-Worlock Estate, ownership by, 61, 69–70, 72–73, 77, 101; heating, 17, 18, 31, 36, 127, 141, 147, 149, 162; heritage structure, non-designation as, 165; lieutenant-governor's residence, 4, 32, 61, 77–91 (*see also* lieutenant-governors); library, 10, 16, 32, 81, 146–47, 149 (*see also* Art Gallery of Greater Victoria: gift shop); location, 8, 9, 37, 49 (*see also* Rockland); morning room, 13, 29, 32–33, 128, 133, 147, 149, 150, 161, 164 (*see also* Art Gallery of Greater Victoria: Massey Gallery; tearoom); names, other: Gyppeswyk, ix, 11; Llan Derwen, ix, 101; porte-cochère, 18, 27, 90, 133, 153–55, 157–158; residents, viii (*see also* Graham, Colin and Sylvia; Green, Alexander and Theophila; McInnes, Thomas and Martha; de Lotbinière, Henri-Gustave and Margaretta Joly; Spencer, David and Emma; Spencer, Sara; Worlock, Frederick and Martha); servants, 32–33, 35–36, 66, 111, 127, 160; subdivision of estate, 14, 37; tiles, 21, 23, 26, 28–29, 31, 149, 151, 164–65, 171 (*see also* Minton, Thomas); trees, Garry oak, 37, 155; views from, 9, 10, 18, 32–33, 36, 49; wallpaper, 29, 33, 147, 150, 164, 172 (*see also* William Morris); water, 17, 36. *See also* Art Gallery of Greater Victoria
Spence-Sales, Harold (architect), 153
Stark, Stuart (architect), 164–65

Symphony, Victoria, 4, 124

Teague, John (architect), 109, 157
Todd, James and Helen (gallery caretakers), 141–42, 159–60, 162
Trounce, Thomas (architect), 56. *See also* Green Block
Trutch, Joseph (lieutenant-governor), 11–12, 81. *See also* Fairfield House
Tupper, Charles Hibbert (politician), 90
Turner, John (premier), 83

Union Club, 104

Verheyden, Charles (architect), 13
Vickrey, William Spencer, 123–124
Victoria Arts Centre. *See* Art Gallery of Greater Victoria
Victoria College, 95, 124
Victoria and Esquimalt Telephone Company, 51, 59
Victoria-Phoenix Brewery, 70
Victoria, Queen, 53, 96

Walton, Frederick (inventor), 33
War, First World, 22, 119, 121, 122, 124
War, Second World, 15, 110, 121–24, 131
War, South African ("Boer"), 84, 95, 122
Worlock Cottage (lieutenant-governor), 71
Wallace, Clarence (lieutenant-governor), 124
Ward, Robert (businessman), 12, 13, 63. *See also* The Laurels
Ward, William Curtis (banker), 13
Wells Fargo Express, 43–44, 47, 55–56, 70, 72, 75. *See also* Garesche Green & Co.
Wilkinson, Robert (reverend), 115. *See also* Methodist Conference
Wilson, Joseph (clothier), 97
Wilson, William (clothier), 97
Women's Canadian Club, 116
Women's Christian Temperance Union, 100, 113, 116
Women's Missionary Society, 113
Worlock Cottage (residence), 71, 182. *See also* Worlock, Frederick
Worlock, Ethel Mary, 68, 75–76
Worlock, Frederick Hammett (banker), 4, 54, 59, 60, 68–73, 86, 99. *See also* Green Worlock & Co.
Worlock, Katharine, 68, 76
Worlock, Martha Amelia Rainer, 60, 69, 70, 74
Worlock, Montague Raymond ("Ray") Clifton, 22, 68, 54, 75, 99
Worlock, Winnifred, 68, 76
Wright & Sanders (architects), 11

Yates, James Stuart (barrister), 72
Young Men's Christian Association (YMCA), 59, 109, 121

ACKNOWLEDGMENTS

I am indebted to a score of people who helped me produce this work. Most important, the Associates of the Art Gallery of Greater Victoria made possible the publication of my research as a book. Also at the Art Gallery of Greater Victoria, Gillian Booth, Bruce Day, Lori Graves, Jen Gretchen, Mary-Jo Hughes, Aldyth Hunter, Diane Rickson, Mary-Ellen Threadkell, Stephen Topfer, and Jon Tupper assisted me faithfully. Special thanks to Judy Thompson whose archival assistance at the gallery was invaluable. Sylvia Graham provided valuable insights into life at the Spencer Mansion in the early 1950s. Professor Martin Segger of the University of Victoria offered encouragement and support. Rosemary James Cross helped me track down the photograph of William Ridgway Wilson, which was graciously provided by Barbara Bishop. Stuart Stark explained anomalies related to the restoration of Gyppeswyk's dining room. Peter Reid took some excellent photographs. Chris Hanna, Sylvia Van Kirk, and Cliff Chandler, members of the Victoria Historical Society, offered invaluable advice. The librarians and archivists at the University of Victoria, the British Columbia Archives, the City of Victoria Archives, and the Greater Victoria Public Library cheerfully answered my questions and directed me to useful materials. Holland Gidney offered skilful editing. Cherry Osborn, Beverley Anne Taylor, and Robert John Taylor provided useful assistance. My wife, Anne, was the first to proofread the manuscript and patiently endured the traditional peccadilloes of a researching and writing historian. Any errors or misconceptions herein are, of course, my own responsibility. Every effort has been made to locate the owners of copyrighted material.

ROBERT RATCLIFFE TAYLOR is the author of several books on German history, as well as the co-author of a number of works on the history of the Welland Canals. He holds a BA in history and English and an MA in history from the University of British Columbia. He also has a PHD with a major in modern European history and minors in medieval and Russian history from Stanford University. After completing his schooling, Robert moved to St. Catharines, Ontario, where he taught European history at Brock University for many years before retiring in 2000. He was also very involved in the community's heritage conservation movement. Since returning with his wife to his hometown of Victoria, BC, in 2003, Rob has served as a docent with the Art Gallery of Greater Victoria, and enjoys giving public tours of the exhibits as well as of the Spencer Mansion.